THE CHURCH LOOKS FORWARD

Books by Dr. William Temple

The Faith and Modern Thought. Six Lectures.

Mens Creatrix. An Essay

Christus Veritas. An Essay

Nature, Man and God. Gifford Lectures, 1932–33 and 1933–34

Readings in St. John's Gospel. (First Series: Chapters I–XII)

Readings in St. John's Gospel. (Second Series: Chapters XIII–XXI)

THE CHURCH
LOOKS FORWARD

BY

WILLIAM TEMPLE

ARCHBISHOP OF CANTERBURY

NEW YORK

THE MACMILLAN COMPANY

1944

PRINTED IN THE UNITED STATES OF AMERICA

PREFACE

IT has been suggested that it might be useful to publish in book form some of the chief sermons and speeches which I delivered during the first eighteen months after entering on my present work. I have decided to follow this advice for two main reasons. One is the hope that they may thus help more effectively the formation of a public opinion ready for action when the opportunity comes; the other is a desire to set those which have already received a good deal of publicity in the context of others which attracted less attention. It is natural that any observations about politics and economics should get a good press; but what I have said on these topics is incidental to, and illustrative of, an exposition of principles which, as I think, should guide our thought in relation to all the great problems of our time.

The addresses here published were delivered on quite different occasions and were in no way planned as a series. In this volume they are so arranged as to exhibit some measure of continuity. They are the chief speeches or addresses which I made during those eighteen months, other than the sermons delivered in parish churches of the diocese.

If any one of these addresses may be said to strike the keynote, it is that on "The Crisis of Western Civilisation". Our need is a new integration of life: Religion, Art, Science, Politics, Education, Industry, Commerce, Finance—all these need to be brought into a unity as agents of a single purpose. That purpose can hardly be found in human aspirations; it must be the divine purpose. That divine purpose is presented to us in the Bible under the name of the Kingdom (Sovereignty) of God, or as the summing-up of all things in Christ, or as the coming-down out of heaven of the holy city, the New Jerusalem.

In all those descriptions two thoughts are prominent: the priority of God and universality of scope. Nothing is to be omitted; "all things" are to be summed up in Christ, but it is in Christ that they are thus gathered into one. All nations are to walk in the light of the holy city, but it comes down out of heaven from God. The Kingdom of God is the goal of human history, but it is His Kingdom, not man's. It is always difficult to think about two or more things at once; but that is what we must learn to do, and these addresses are essays in that enterprise.

WILLIAM CANTUAR:

January 25, 1944

CONTENTS

THE CHURCH LOOKS FORWARD

I

Enthronement

THE SERMON PREACHED AT THE ENTHRONEMENT
IN CANTERBURY CATHEDRAL ON ST. GEORGE'S DAY, 1942

The nations shall walk by the light thereof.
Revelation xxi. 24

AT such a moment as this it is inevitable that we should have in our minds the background against which our day of dedication is set. For, of course, the real meaning of this day is dedication—the dedication of the Church, of the nation, of ourselves, to the service of the Most High God. It is fitting that it should be held on St. George's Day and that with the martyr who is patron saint of our country we should here, in the mother Church of the Anglican Communion, reaffirm our loyalty to Jesus Christ as alone entitled to our absolute allegiance. My chief desire is to enter on my office as His bondman and His witness; and I ask of you all to hold me to this by your own stedfastness and by your prayers.

The world is learning its helplessness apart from God, though not yet is it on any great scale turning to Him for direction or for strength. The secular movement of the world is not towards peace or mutual understanding and appreciation; rather is it towards more intense and fiercer competition, conflict and war between larger and ever larger concentrations of power. That power may be economic or military or both;

1

but the movement towards greater concentrations of power and keener tension between them is the mark of our period of history.

. If that were all that could be said, the Church could do little else but work below the surface, morally if not physically returning to the catacombs, preserving the Gospel in its purity and potential might, until it again confronts the world as the one coherent fellowship which can alone give stability and peace to a world relapsing into chaos. But there is another side to the picture. As though in preparation for such a time as this, God has been building up a Christian fellowship which now extends into almost every nation, and binds citizens of them all together in true unity and mutual love. No human agency has planned this. It is the result of the great missionary enterprise of the last hundred and fifty years. Neither the missionaries nor those who sent them out were aiming at the creation of a world-wide fellowship interpenetrating the nations, bridging the gulfs between them, and supplying the promise of a check to their rivalries. The aim for nearly the whole period was to preach the Gospel to as many individuals as could be reached so that those who were won to discipleship should be put in the way of eternal salvation. Almost incidentally the great world-fellowship has arisen; it is the great new fact of our era; it makes itself apparent from time to time in World Conferences such as in the last twenty years have been held in Stockholm, Lausanne, Jerusalem, Oxford, Edinburgh, Madras, Amsterdam.

The New Testament bids us hope for a City of God whose gates are ever open to the four points of the compass so that all may enter, and that the nations shall walk by the light of it. That City in its perfection is of eternity and not of time; but, as the central doctrine of our faith assures us, it is God's will that the things of time should, as far as may be, represent to us the eternal realities. We may not hope for the Kingdom of God in its completeness here, but we are to pray for its coming and to live even now as its citizens. And here we find ourselves actually belonging to a fellowship which is an earthly counterpart of that City of God, though many of us are hardly aware of it and all of us are frequently forgetful of it. The City of God, which has sometimes appeared as a beleagured fortress, again stands before us with gates wide open so that citizens of all nations may enter, but also that its own citizens may ride forth to the conquest of the nations, following their Captain as He goes forth to judge and to make war.

Yes; here is one great ground of hope for the coming days —this world-wide Christian fellowship, this ecumenical movement, as it is often called. And that is part of the background of this day's act of dedication as truly as the conflict of nations and the war which for the time, till victory is won, claims our utmost energy.

This is not the moment to say much about the war; but a German victory, in Germany's present mood, would mean the end of that ecumenical Christian movement and all the hopes connected with it. This is no guess; it is the declared policy of the German State and follows of necessity from its principles. It is our duty as Christian citizens to do our utmost towards winning the war that we may keep open the possibility of a Christian civilisation and maintain the hope of a fellowship pervading all nations under the allegiance of Jesus our Lord. Of this hope itself more may well be said because it is so near the heart of our purpose here to-day.

St. Paul saw the Church as the fellowship in which all earthly divisions are abolished; neither religious tradition, nor education, nor economic status, nor even sex, can make division there; "there is neither Jew nor Gentile, neither Greek nor barbarian, neither bond nor free, neither male nor female; but one man in Christ Jesus". No doubt the members of the Church have in the course of history failed signally to manifest to the world this unity which always marks the living Church itself. And the reason is not chiefly lack of good feeling among themselves, for this is the symptom, not the disease. The reason is the incompleteness of our self-surrender to the one Lord.

But now, out of the great missionary movement with its proclamation of the Gospel of the love of God and its call for self-surrender as our response to that Gospel, is arising, on a scale never before seen in the world, the Christian fellowship which corresponds to St. Paul's description. It is of urgent importance that we become aware of it, that we further it in every way open to us, and that through it we take our part in providing for the Spirit of Christ the agency by which He may transform the world.

But we, who are assembled here, are not only individuals offering our service to the world-wide fellowship of Christian disciples, we are—with some honoured guests representing that wider fellowship—members of the Anglican Communion, met in the mother Church of that Communion, to set in St. Augustine's seat one more in the long line of his successors. We shall impoverish our service of the wider fellowship if we let our membership of our own Communion become hesitant or indefinite. Rather we have to make strong the bonds of our own unity, with gratitude for our splendid inheritance, so that we may bring to the universal Church a life strong in faith, in order, in corporate devotion—maintaining all that we have received but recognising also God's gifts to His people through traditions other than our own.

So let us set ourselves to gain a deepening loyalty to our Anglican tradition of Catholic order, Evangelical immediacy in our approach to God, and liberal acceptance of new truth made known to us; and let us at the same time join with all our fellow Christians who will join with us in bearing witness to the claim of Christ to rule in every department of human life, and to the principles of His Kingdom.

Thus we come back to our starting point. We are representatives and trustees of that light which more than anything else the world is needing, and which can guide our feet into the way of peace. But we can be effective representatives and faithful trustees only in proportion as our hearts and minds and wills are given to Him who is Himself the day-spring from on high. To dedicate ourselves afresh to Him and to His service in our own time is the real purpose of our presence here.

At almost any other moment in the history of the world I should have wished my words at such a service to be concerned with this alone—God's call to us and our answering dedication. At this moment it seemed right to recall the state of the world in which our service must be given. Yet let not this obscure the primary need—hearts open to the love of God, minds nurtured by the truth of God, wills devoted to the purpose of God.

As I try with you so to open my heart, to nurture my mind and to devote my will, in face of the task entrusted to me, you will forgive a few personal words expressing my sense of complete inadequacy to perform that task or worthily to follow those whom I have known as the occupants of this see. This first was Edward White Benson, deep and subtle scholar, wise statesman and true priest. Then came my own father, of whom I say nothing except that he was and is, among men, the chief inspiration of my life; and I like here to recall two sayings at his own enthronement, one a quotation from his predecessor and former college tutor, Archibald Campbell Tait—Nobis Apostolorum vindicamus non honores, sed labores—We claim for ourselves the Apostles' labours, not their honours; the other his own words: "I would rather that my intimate friends knew me as one who thought nothing of himself in comparison of the work that he had to do than that they should know me as a great scholar or a great saint". He was followed by Randall Thomas Davidson, a man of comprehensive wisdom illuminated by direct and simple faith, who became almost at once a second father to me, and whose vast influence upon the whole Anglican Communion is a priceless treasure in our inheritance. Lastly, Cosmo Gordon Lang, who, since I first knew him forty-one years ago, has been to me a most wise elder counsellor and ever more intimate friend. His high sense of duty has led him to lay down an office in which he was still giving great service to Church and nation, but we rejoice that his store of wisdom is still available for our guidance.

To follow such men is daunting. If even what is obvious of the task in prospect did not fill one with a sense of helplessness, the memory of those in whose place I stand would abolish all self-confidence. Yet that is gain and not loss. Our chief need is an ever revitalised apprehension of the completeness of our dependence upon God. I have spoken of the meaning of this service as being our dedication of the Church, the nation, ourselves to the purpose of God. But that, though true in its measure, does not go far enough. For dedication is an activity of our wills, necessary but not ultimate. The chief need of all is that we here and now let our dependence upon

God become so living a fact of actual experience that we may be from henceforth channels of His living energy.

This, then, is my call to you to-day, and, beyond you who are gathered here, to all whom my words may reach: Just because our hope is set on that City in whose light the nations shall walk, let us abide in Christ that Christ may abide in us.

Let us kneel in prayer. And as we kneel let us try to hear the familiar words of the Lord as though hearing them now for the first time: "Abide in me and I in you. As the branch cannot bear fruit of itself except it abide in the vine; no more can ye except ye abide in me. I am the vine, ye are the branches. He that abideth in me and I in him, the same bringeth forth much fruit; for apart from me ye can do nothing. . . . Herein is my Father glorified, that ye bear much fruit."

Now unto him that is able to do exceeding abundantly above all that we ask or think, according to the power that worketh in us, to him be glory in the Church and in Christ Jesus unto all generations for ever and ever. AMEN.

II

Christian Unity and Church Reunion

THE PRESIDENTIAL ADDRESS DELIVERED IN FULL SYNOD
TO THE CONVOCATION OF CANTERBURY
ON TUESDAY, MAY 25TH, 1943

RIGHT Reverend, Very Reverend, Venerable and Reverend Brethren,—It is recommended by the Committee on our procedure that it would be advantageous if the Presidential Address were delivered in Full Synod. I have decided to act on this without waiting for our consideration of that Committee's report, because if the Presidential Address is delivered only in the Upper House a very long delay is inevitable before the members of the Lower House can become aware of the full text of it. Moreover I value highly the opportunity of even this limited meeting in one place as a means by which our sense of fellowship in the service of Christ and His Church may be deepened.

We meet at a moment of tense interest and keen anticipation. We share with all our countrymen profound gratitude for the triumphs won by our fleets and armies and air force, and by those of our Allies. And with renewed devotion we commend our cause to God, praying that we may be worthy to serve it and carry it to victory, and so guided by the Holy Spirit as to meet worthily the great responsibilities which victory must bring.

As I turn to our own immediate business as a Synod of the Church I find myself obliged to take this opportunity of speaking about Christian Unity and Church Reunion. I have rather shrunk from doing this, because it may fall to me later to speak on behalf of this Synod as representing the Province of Canterbury in the Universal Church; and I sincerely wish to keep my mind open to the arguments that may be presented to us in discussions which are likely to take place in the near future. But I also feel responsibility for offering to the Church such guidance as I can from my experience—very brief as yet—in the office which I now hold, from fourteen years' service as Chairman of the Faith and Order Movement, and from thirty-one years' service of that Movement as one chosen by the Archbishops of our Church to represent it in conference with members of other communions.

First I would say something about Christian unity and co-operation of such a kind as is possible while our ecclesiastical divisions remain. Of this the Religion and Life Weeks are an illustration. Experience shews beyond any possibility of dispute that there is a readiness in the public to pay attention to the Christian message when Christians of all communions are united in proclaiming it entirely beyond any that can be commanded when we deliver it in separation from one another. The first striking manifestation of this was provided by the two great meetings in the Stoll Picture House presided over, the one by Cardinal Hinsley and the other by my predecessor, Archbishop Lord Lang. We now have a joint-committee to facilitate co-operation in witness between the British Council of Churches and the Roman Catholic Sword of the Spirit.

That there is need for the most effective witness to Christian moral and social principles is very plain. The Christian tradition is challenged from without more powerfully than in any period since the end of the Dark Ages, and is in danger of being undermined by a secular humanism which hopes to retain Christian values without Christian faith. If then there is special need for effective Christian witness, and if one condition of maximum effectiveness is that we give that witness unitedly, a refusal or failure to unite for this purpose would be a betrayal of trust; it would be a refusal or failure to serve not only the people of our generation but our Lord Himself.

No doubt there are principles to be observed and safeguarded, and we must so plan our united witness as not to break or compromise them. At this point there may be some disagreement among us; in my view the proper place at which to draw the line while the relations between the various communions remain as they are, is where it is drawn in the resolutions of the Upper House now to be considered in the Lower House. Until we have reached that consummation of union which will consist in full sacramental communion, it would seem to me wrong and false to admit as a preacher during the service of Holy Communion one who belongs to another communion than our own. On the other hand, to admit such a one to preach the sermon appended to Morning or Evening Prayer on the occasion of any enterprise of united witness seems to me appropriate and most desirable. If the occasions for interchange of preachers are limited to special services, the impression of truly united witness is greatly impaired; and this should be avoided unless it is held that some really vital principle is at stake. I find it hard to see how this could be.

So far I have been speaking of united witness to Christian faith and principles in such fields as Christian Evidence, Apologetics or the subjects commonly included in a Religion and Life Week; these are Religion in the Home, Religion in the School, Religion in Industry and Commerce, and Religion in International Relations.

The Lambeth Conference of 1930 also expressly encouraged Joint-Evangelism. Experience shews that this is far more difficult. If two speakers representing different communions have proclaimed the Gospel and appealed for personal decisions, an awkward situation arises when one of their hearers declares himself convinced and asks what he does next. Which speaker is to direct him? This difficulty can be avoided by the method followed with great effect, as I am assured, in South London and some other places. This is the method of a united evangelistic campaign conducted in parallel services, but opened with a united service of prayer and closing with a united service of thanksgiving and dedication. Thus each preacher proclaims the truth as he has been able to see it with sharp outlines and clear direction to those whose hearts are touched; and yet there is the added power of witness due to the fact that all the local representatives of Christianity are co-operating, and manifestly regard each other as colleagues in a common service of one Lord, fighting as allies in the warfare against the world, the flesh and the devil, and not as rivals or enemies to one another.

For we must see our divisions and consider the problems created by our divisions against the background of the paganism of the unconverted, whether overseas or in our own country. At every turn our divisions hinder our service. They blunt our appeal to the general public at home or to the adherents of other religions abroad. They prevent the Government from offering facilities which it would readily offer to a united Church, and does offer now with greater readiness when we can put forward a united claim.

Worst of all, our divisions render flatly impossible any

complete fulfilment of the primary purpose of the Church—effective witness to the One God and to the fellowship, despite all causes of severance, which can hold together in one the disciples of Christ. How can we persuade an incredulous world that we have the secret of that unity which overleaps all barriers of religious or cultural inheritance, of economic status or of sex itself, so that we become "one man in Christ Jesus", if we present to that world the appearance of competing sects? The obligation to attain to a real and organic unity of the Church as the Holy Spirit may guide us is urgent; yet it is to be feared that many Church-people are almost unaware of it and indifferent to it.

Yet we are trustees for certain truths, as we with complete conviction hold them to be, which we must bring to the united Church of the future as that part of its treasure which has been committed to us. I ask your leave to put before you the considerations in the light of which it seems to me that we should approach any projected Scheme of Reunion, whether that now under consideration in India or any other.

If I refer to the South Indian Scheme it will be by way of illustration only. It would be idle to pretend that I have a completely unformed or an empty mind on that subject. I have inevitably thought much about it and have formed provisionally some conclusions. But I am honestly trying to weigh all arguments that may be presented to me and to avoid becoming irrevocably committed to any judgment until I have to speak, if that later on becomes my duty, in the name of this Synod and the Province for which it may be called upon to act. My provisional judgment will probably appear in what I say; but it is provisional and my aim is not to utter my own opinion but to offer what material I can to the Church as it seeks to exercise a right judgment in this important matter.

We should, I think, approach the question whether or not a particular scheme of union is acceptable with the conviction that the fundamental anomaly is that any two disciples of our Lord should not be in communion with one another. We are so used to this state of things that we seldom pause to appreciate its gravity. I would urge that we try to recover in some measure the horror of divisions among Christians which is evident in St. Paul. It does not follow that we shall at once agree to any scheme of union rather than perpetuate disunion, for, as I have said, we are trustees for an apprehension of truth which we have to bring into the treasury of the united Church. But our initial disposition will be towards effecting union if we can without disloyalty to truth, rather than towards so emphasising our distinctive tradition as to make the accomplishment of union harder than it is bound in any case to be.

Next we shall remember two facts concerning schism. The first is that while schism is undoubtedly a sinful state, being contrary to the declared purpose of God, yet schism is within the Church, the Body of Christ, and does not effect separation from it as do apostasy and infidelity. The second is that, sinful as schism is, there is no guilt of schism in those who are loyal to the teaching which they have received, still less in those who have been converted from heathenism by missionaries of one or another of our sadly manifold traditions. It is one of the greatest evils of our divisions that they are reproduced in the experience of converts who have no responsibility for them.

Against the background of such reflections we have to consider any actual proposal for union. It is, of course, conceivable that this should take the form of an approach on the part of a body separated from ourselves with readiness to accept in its entirety our whole system of Faith and Order as we have ourselves received it. But this is most unlikely. Individuals may transfer their spiritual allegiance; but it is hardly to be expected that whole communions will at any time be found ready to accept the whole system of some other communion. If there is desire for union, but not readiness for that complete acceptance, negotiations are inevitable; these are bound to take the form of mutual adjustment, and each uniting body, before consenting to the scheme, is called upon to satisfy itself that the essential principles of its own tradition are sufficiently embodied in the scheme. And in the process of forming a judgment on any scheme regard must be had to two different questions: (1) Is the scheme for the united Church, as it is to be, satisfactory? (2) Is the mode of transition so designed as to avoid any fatal compromise of principle?

As regards the first of these questions, it is to be expected that the scheme will not be precisely what any of the negotiating parties in isolation would have prepared. In our negotiations with any of the non-episcopal communions the main point of difficulty is bound to concern the Ministry.

The Lambeth Conference has repeatedly offered as a basis of negotiation the famous Quadrilateral. This appears in the celebrated Appeal to all Christian People issued by the Conference of 1920, in the form—

The Holy Scriptures, as the record of God's revelation of Himself to man, and as being the rule and ultimate standard of faith; and the Creed commonly called Nicene, as the sufficient statement of the Christian faith, and either it or the Apostles' Creed as the Baptismal Confession of belief:

The divinely instituted sacraments of Baptism and the Holy Communion, as expressing for all the corporate life of the whole fellowship in and with Christ;

A ministry acknowledged by every part of the Church as possessing not only the inward call of the Spirit, but also the commission of Christ and the authority of the whole body.[1]

As regards the Holy Scriptures, the Creeds as formulations of the faith of the Church, and the two Dominical Sacraments, there is a very large general agreement between the Anglican Churches and those with whom Anglicans in England, in India and elsewhere have been holding conversations or negotiations with a view to union. No doubt it is our duty, before action is taken, to be satisfied that this agreement is genuine. My own view is that no serious question would have been raised about this if there were not anxieties in many quarters with regard to the proposals affecting the Ministry. It is perfectly reasonable that anxiety with regard to one part of a scheme should occasion special care with regard to other parts; for if it is doubtfully satisfactory at one point it is all the more important that it should be unquestionably satisfactory at others. None the less, I believe it to be the fact that questions with regard to the other three elements in the Quadrilateral are secondary in the sense that they would not be pressed in relation to any of the schemes actually under or in process of consideration unless there were anxiety concerning the Ministry; and this anxiety is felt both with regard to the scheme itself and with regard to the transitional period.

I think it would be improper that I should at this stage express my own judgment on these points. I am concerned here as elsewhere to describe the background against which I think it should be formed. Part of that background is the large measure of agreement with regard to the Ministry expressed both in the World Conferences on Faith and Order at

[1] Bell, *Documents on Christian Unity*, I, p. 3.

Lausanne in 1927 and at Edinburgh in 1937, and in the Joint Conferences held at Lambeth Palace as a result of the Lambeth Appeal in 1920. Thus on May 29th, 1922, the Anglican and Free Church representatives agreed in adopting the following propositions:

1. A Ministry of the Word and Sacraments is a Divine ordinance for the Church, and has been since the days of the Apostles an integral part of its organised life.
2. It is a ministry within the Church, exercising representatively, in the Name and by the authority of the Lord Who is the Head of the Church, the powers and functions which are inherent in the Church.
3. It is a ministry of the Church, and not merely of any part thereof.
4. No man can take this ministry upon himself. It must be conferred by the Church, acting through those who have authority given to them in the Church to confer it. There must be not only an inward call of the Spirit, but also an outward and visible call and commission by the Church.
5. It is in accordance with Apostolic practice and the ancient custom of the Church that the commission should be given through Ordination, with prayer and the laying on of hands by those who have authority given to them to ordain.
6. We believe that in Ordination, together with this commission to minister, Divine Grace is given through the Holy Spirit in response to prayer and faith for the fulfilment of the charge so committed.
   (Para. 7 refers to the divergences of the forms of ministry and expresses the need for a ministry "acknowledged by every part [of the Church] as possessing the authority of the whole body".)
8. In view of the fact that the Episcopate was from early times and for many centuries accepted, and by the great part of Christendom is still accepted, as the means whereby the authority of the whole body is given, we agree that it

ought to be accepted as such for the United Church of the future.

9. Similarly, in view of the place which the Council of Presbyters and the Congregation of the faithful had in the constitution of the early Church, and the preservation of these elements of presbyterial and congregational order in large sections of Christendom, we agree that they should be maintained with a representative and constitutional Episcopate as permanent elements in the order and life of the United Church.

10. The acceptance of Episcopal Ordination for the future would not imply the acceptance of any particular theory as to its origin or character, or the disowning of past ministries of Word and Sacrament otherwise received, which have, together with those received by Episcopal Ordination, been used and blessed by God.[1]

I have quoted those propositions partly because of the weight attaching to the names of the Anglican and Free Church representatives who adopted them—I shall give the Anglican names shortly in another connection—and partly because they set forth a doctrine of the Ministry which many Anglicans are unaware that the great body of Free Church theologians accept. Indeed I have heard members of the House of Clergy—whether or not of this Convocation I will not say —attribute to Free Churchmen theories of the Ministry which, in fact, they vehemently repudiate. And I have quoted the English terms of agreement rather than the Indian, because I wish to avoid any appearance of discussing more than one or two points in the Indian proposals.

But it is plain that those proposals seek to embody the principles set out in the English resolutions. Those resolutions have not been endorsed by any Synod and have no formal

[1] Bell, *Documents on Christian Unity*, I, pp. 148–50.

authority. But they have great moral weight, and we should be slow to reject any scheme which embodies them satisfactorily. They point clearly to a bringing together in one system of the Episcopal, Presbyteral and Congregational principles; and that, broadly speaking, is the aim of the South India Scheme. I will here refer to two points only in that scheme.

First, it provides that Ordination shall in future be episcopal. That is, of course, from our standpoint indispensable. It is true that the United Church would be free to recognise other ministries not only during the interim period but beyond it; probably this is wise; people are more likely to accept fully and with conviction a system which they may freely modify than one which is supposedly irreversible. Freedom allows prejudices to die down. And of course it is in fact impossible to bind the next generation.

Secondly, there is the provision in the scheme whereby the Episcopate can be overruled even on matters of doctrine by the other members of the Synod. The question is raised whether in such a case the Episcopate with its historical functions is really incorporated into the scheme. It is much to be regretted that the scheme contains this provision. But it is not true to say that no special place is given to the Episcopate in this matter; the elaborate safeguards contained in the scheme are a recognition of the special responsibility of the Episcopate as the guardian of the faith. Whether this should be regarded as sufficient if at this stage it is a necessary price of unity, is one of the matters calling for consideration. With the possible exception of the point just mentioned, it is true, I think, that the scheme retains the essentials of Catholic Order with regard to the Ministry so far as concerns its permanent provisions.

I turn for a few moments to the Interim provisions. In the English conversations the main point of difficulty has concerned the transition. It has been generally agreed that the Free Churches cannot and ought not to repudiate their own spiritual ancestry. But beyond that agreement has not been reached. I will ask leave to recall the main statements from the Anglican side which bear upon this.

The Lambeth Appeal, after claiming that the Episcopate is the one means of providing a universally acknowledged Ministry, went on to say:

It is not that we call in question for a moment the spiritual reality of the ministries of those communions which do not possess the Episcopate. On the contrary we thankfully acknowledge that these ministries have been manifestly blessed and owned by the Holy Spirit as effective means of grace.

In the conversations afterwards held at Lambeth those expressions were amplified in a memorandum contributed by the Anglican representatives; in view of its importance I give their names, which evidently carry great weight: Archbishop Davidson of Canterbury; Archbishop Lang of York; Bishop Winnington Ingram of London; Bishop Talbot of Winchester; Bishop Chase of Ely; Bishop Kempthorne of Lichfield; Bishop Woods of Peterborough; Bishop Strong of Ripon; Bishop Donaldson of Salisbury; Bishop Headlam of Gloucester; Bishop Gibson, lately of Gloucester; and Dr. W. H. Frere, afterwards Bishop of Truro. Their memorandum was presented on July 6th, 1923.

These Anglican representatives first make it clear that they have no authority to give an official interpretation of the Appeal; they then explain that the ministries of which they speak are non-espiscopal ministries which rest upon a long-established order, which have been conferred by some solemn and authoritative act implying Ordination to the ministry of the Universal Church and not merely commission to the ministry of a particular denomination, and which are regarded as involving a lifelong vocation.

Concerning such ministries these Anglican representatives write as follows:

Such Free Church ministries we find it impossible to regard as "invalid", that is, as null and void, or as effecting none of the purposes for which the ministry has been Divinely ordained in the Church of Christ. . . . We consider that we are entitled, by manifest tokens of Divine blessing which these ministries possess, and also by the spirit and terms of the Lambeth Appeal about them, to go further and to say that we regard them as being within their several spheres real ministries in the Universal Church. . . . It seems to us to be in accordance with the Lambeth Appeal to say, as we are prepared to say, that the ministries which we have in view in this memorandum, ministries which imply a sincere intention to preach Christ's word and administer the Sacraments as Christ has ordained, and to which authority so to do has been solemnly given by the Church concerned, are real ministries of Christ's Word and Sacraments in the Universal Church.[1]

The Anglican representatives did not stop there, and in a moment we shall attend to what they went on to say. But, being who they were, they said that: and inevitably their words made a great impression.

To me it seems to be a primary question in this connection whether or not we are entitled to form such a judgment. Are we entitled to say of any ministry transmitted by other than the channels familiar for centuries to the whole Church, that they have been "blessed and owned by the Holy Spirit" and

[1] Bell, *Documents on Christian Unity,* I, pp. 158, 159.

are "within their several spheres real ministries in the Universal Church"? I cannot doubt that we are both entitled and obliged to make such a judgment. And if we thus judge that the Holy Spirit has blessed and owned these ministries, can we without presumption and profanity refuse to recognise them ourselves?

Many unnecessary difficulties are caused, as I believe, by a readiness to draw negative inferences from positive premises. We have our own grounds of complete assurance that the Ministry which we have received is of God. We must at least be very cautious how we conclude that where those grounds of assurance are lacking, the Ministry which lacks them is not of God. We should rightly refuse to accept them for ourselves so long as there is no effective intention to heal the breach and restore the universally acknowledged Ministry on the basis of what we know as ground of complete assurance. In other words, we cannot in practice recognise what we must regard as irregular ministries, however effective within their own spheres, until there is an operative decision to unite in a way that ends the irregularity. But when that is present, ought we not to be ready to recognise during a period of transition what God has blessed and owned until the new rule is generally established and all ministers have been episcopally ordained?

The Anglican representatives followed the words lately quoted with these: "Yet ministries even when so regarded, may be in varying degrees irregular or defective". They then quote the Preface to the Ordinal and continue as follows:

Thus the Angelican Church is bound to secure the authorisation of its ministers for its own congregations, and no one could be authorised to exercise his ministry among them who had not been episcopally ordained. . . .

(1) We regard the rule quoted above as much more than a rule of internal discipline. It embodies principles to which the Anglican Church has throughout its history adhered, and which contribute to the special position which it claims to hold in the Catholic Church.

(2) We cannot lose sight of the relations in which we stand to other Episcopal Churches in East and West; nor can we ignore the danger of creating pain and disturbance, or even the possibility of schism, within our own communion if the rule and principle contained in the Ordinal were to be set aside.[1]

The Anglican representatives then went on to recommend conditional Ordination.

The words just quoted raise the point dealt with in the South India Scheme in the section known as the Gentlemen's Agreement. About this I am prepared to say without hesitation that when the Lambeth Conference of 1930 encouraged the Church in India, Burma and Ceylon to go forward with the scheme, it certainly interpreted that section as meaning that a non-episcopally-ordained minister would not be appointed to the charge of a previously Anglican Church except in the rarest circumstances which would be such as to afford a manifest ground for exceptional action; as an illustration I might mention the possibility that a congregation of very simple converts were left without a minister, perhaps through the death of their own pastor, and that no Anglican minister was available. In such a case the pastoral urgency might well be regarded as overriding any irregularity involved.

And pastoral urgency is a main factor in the whole situation. The missions of the various communions have inevitably developed on a geographical basis; so one district, so far as it is Christian at all, is almost entirely Anglican,

[1] Bell, *Documents on Christian Unity,* I, pp. 159, 160.

another almost entirely Methodist and so on. But the mobility of the people steadily increases as the conditions of life are modernised. When a Methodist convert from Mysore comes into an Anglican district in Madras, is he to be received or repelled? When an Anglican convert goes from Madras to a Methodist district in Mysore, is he to continue his sacramental practice or abandon it? He is, perhaps, a simple and unsophisticated person. If he can join fully with the Christian congregation where he lives, he will grow in discipleship as the years pass; but if he has in any way to hold aloof, and that for reasons which must be obscure to him, he is likely to relapse into the Hinduism which surrounds him with its peculiar power of suction. Plainly the worshippers must move freely from one communion to another. Yet if that is permitted without some scheme of union, we shall be giving away our principles with both hands.

The decision rests, not with us, but with the Church of India, Burma and Ceylon. It may be that I shall receive from the Metropolitan of India some questions which he will request me to answer on behalf of this Province. If so, the process of arriving at the answer to be sent must be settled with reference to the content of the questions. But of course in one way or another, both Houses of Convocation will be consulted and the answer framed in the light of that consultation.

Whatever decision is reached in India will in no way affect our position in England. The Lambeth Conference of 1930 carried the following resolution, to which I have no doubt that this Convocation would give its assent; it is Resolution 40(d):

The Conference thinks it wise to point out that, after the union in South India has been inaugurated, both ministers and lay people of the united Church, when they are outside the jurisdiction of that Church, will be amenable to the regulations of the Province and Diocese in which they desire to officiate or to worship, and it must be assumed that those regulations will be applied to individuals in the same manner as they would now be applied to similarly circumstanced individuals, unless any Province takes formal action to change its regulations.

There are of course many points in the South India Scheme which call for scrutiny in addition to those which I have mentioned. I have touched on these only to illustrate the spirit in which, and the background against which, I think such a scheme should be considered. As so often there are two duties, each relatively easy to fulfil in isolation, not easy to combine; they may be expressed in two apostolic injunctions which themselves are offered in combination: "Quench not the spirit; hold fast that which is good".

As I have no doubt that the inclination of my own present judgment has been apparent, though I hold myself ready to reconsider the whole matter and have rather asked questions than answered them, let me conclude this address, already I fear too long, with a personal confession of faith concerning the Ministry to which you and I have been called.

When we go back to the first records of the Church we find neither a Ministry which called people into association with it, nor an undifferentiated fellowship which delegated powers to a Ministry; but we find a complete Church, with the Apostolate accepted as its focus of administration and authority. When the Lord's earthly ministry was ended, there was found in the world as its fruit and as means of its continuance this Body, in which the distinction of Ministry and Laity is already established. The Apostles were in no sense ministers of the laity; they were ministers of Christ to the laity, and to the world waiting to be won. They took steps for the perpetuation of the Ministry, and it has descended to ourselves. So when I consecrate a godly and well-learned man to the office and work of a Bishop in the Church of God, I do not act as a representative of the Church, if by that is meant the whole number of contemporary Christians; but I do act as the ministerial instrument of Christ in His Body the Church. The authority by which I act is His, transmitted to me through His Apostles and those to whom they committed it; I hold it neither from the Church nor apart from the Church, but from Christ in the Church. I was myself admitted to the episcopate by the twofold succession—succession in office and succession of consecration. The two streams of succession are different from the point where they converged upon me; but as we trace them back they meet again at some point previous to Gregory who sent Augustine and Vergilius who consecrated him; and so the double line runs back to apostolic times.

This authority to consecrate and to ordain is itself witness to the continuity of the life of the Church in its unceasing dependence on its Head, Jesus Christ, who is the same yesterday and to-day and for ever. Every priest who by virtue of his Ordination celebrates the Holy Communion acts not for the congregation there present, nor for all Christian people then living on the earth, but as the organ of the Body of Christ, the ministerial instrument of Christ active in and through His Body; so that though no more than two or three persons be actually assembled, yet the congregation at that Holy Communion service is the Communion of Saints, with which the persons present, be they few or many, are there conjoined. Here therefore, as in the Incarnation itself, we find the eternal in the midst of time, the secret of a fellowship against which the gates of death cannot prevail.

It is possible to hold such a faith without the sacramental expression of it in the Apostolic Ministry; but those who by God's election have received that Ministry will neither surrender it nor so hold it as to make difficult the access of others to it. We hold it as a treasure and a trust. It is our duty both to safeguard it and to commend it, both to preserve it for ourselves and our children, and to make easy the way of entering into participation in it, provided only that in making our treasure available we do not dissipate or squander it.

III

The Background of the Reunion Problem

AN ADDRESS DELIVERED TO THE CANTERBURY DIOCESAN
CONFERENCE ON MONDAY, JULY 19TH, 1943

THE discussion of the South India Scheme has brought the whole question of reunion into prominence, and I should like to take this opportunity of discussing what seem to me some of the fundamental considerations, not of this scheme in particular, but of the reunion movement in general; and first let us recall the fact that the unity of the Church is essential to the complete discharge of its commission. It is called to give witness to the One God and to the hope of universal fellowship for all mankind in His service. Plainly it cannot do either of these things effectively if it is itself divided and therefore fails to be itself the fellowship into which it calls the various nations and the many sections within the nations. Yet it may be that the difficulty of maintaining and now re-establishing unity is due in part to an over-exclusive emphasis upon the importance of unity as compared with variety; at any rate it is true that this unity is, in musical terms, one of harmony, not of unison. St. Paul's favourite analogy is that of the body, which has one life but many limbs, and all the limbs are different. The life of the body requires every one of them for the fulness of its own expression, and it requires each in its own appropriate place: the loss of any limb imposes a limitation on the body as a whole: the independent activity of any limb

27

is a symptom not of health but of paralysis; and if it were possible that a limb should get into the wrong place, as for example a hand at the end of a leg or a foot at the end of an arm, its utility would be ruined. The unity of the body is a harmony of many parts, each discharging its own function in relation to a single life.

But the One Body of Christ has been mutilated throughout its history. Its first mutilation was not a division of the Christian Church but was the failure of Israel to allow itself to take its part in the reconstituted people of God. Let us consider for a moment the enormous difference that would have been made if Israel had responded in considerable measure to the call of Christ: during the formative period of the first five centuries, the strongly philosophical tendency of Greek culture would have been balanced by the prophetic note derived from the Hebrew tradition, and while I do not for a moment suppose that this would have modified the doctrinal formulations of the Church, I think it certain that the whole temper and ethos of the Church would have been different, inasmuch as the ethical concern would have been developed in a more adequate proportion to the concern about orthodoxy of doctrine. There was one of its proper limbs over which the Body never gained control and it has suffered throughout its history from the lack.

The first great division within the Church itself was that between East and West. The Eastern Church carried forward the philosophical tradition of Greek culture, with the result that it has had a capacity for adjustment and flexibility, gathered up under its general doctrine of economy, which makes it in many ways more sympathetic towards those who are in one way or another detached from it than the Church of the West has tended to be; but it has at the same time lacked the effectiveness and the capacity for organisation which have always been strong in any community deriving its tradition primarily from Rome. The Western Church on the other hand has been organised to a great pitch of effectiveness in action but has in the process tended to lack intellectual and moral sympathy. This became all the more marked so far as the Latin Church is concerned when the division of East and West was followed some four centuries later by the division of North and South: the strong Teutonic tradition of local self-government was detached from the Roman tendency towards centralisation, with the result that the Roman system became harder still, while the Protestant North, for lack of what Rome could contribute, tended to break up into a welter of competing sects.

In other words, we cannot avoid the conclusion that every division involves loss on both sides; each is the poorer for lack of what it might have learnt from that body of Christians that has become separated from it.

Moreover, in the controversy which inevitably develops there arises a disproportionate attention to those points which have given rise to the separation. Instead of these being seen and appreciated only in their proper perspective in the life of the whole body, they attract undue attention to themselves. If for example we compare that succession in the Ministry, which we hold as a treasure for ourselves to enjoy and for large parts of Christendom to receive one day, as we hope, from us, with the spinal system of the human body, we become aware at once that a healthy man thinks very little about his spine: it is true that its importance cannot be exaggerated, but as long as it is functioning properly he hardly gives it a thought: his attention can be given to the purpose which the body and all its members exist to serve. So some of our attention has been diverted from the service of God, which it is the Church's function to render, to a concern about this ministerial spine of our system. It would be much wholesomer if we could take it for granted; but that will be impossible until it is universally accepted.

If all this is true, what can we say about the way of recovery? First, we need surely to take care that all Christian people are joining together in their service of God and man to the utmost extent that the actual unity among them permits. Whatever purpose there is that we have in common, let us pursue together; let us act to the full on the basis of our actual unity. Recent developments, especially the establishment of the World Council of Churches and of the British Council of Churches, provide for us new opportunities for this.

Secondly, in our dealings with one another let us be more eager to understand those who differ from us than either to refute them or to press upon them our own tradition. Our whole manner of speech and conduct, and of course supremely our mode of worship, will inevitably give expression to our own tradition. Wherever there are divisions which persist, there is sure to be something of value on both sides. We ought always to be eager to learn the truth which others possess in fuller degree than ourselves, and to learn why some give to various elements in our common belief a greater emphasis than we are accustomed to give. Our temper in conference must be rather that of learners than that of champions.

And yet with both of these there must be full loyalty to the truth as we have been enabled to apprehend it. Otherwise we shall have no contribution to bring and shall have squandered the treasure that we hold in trust for the united Church of future days. And we must expect others to be similarly loyal to their own apprehension of truth. So we shall respect one another's consciences, and even though there may be sadness, there will never be resentment because at some point we find it impossible, until fuller understanding is reached, to exhibit to the world the full unity which alone bears witness to the truth we are called to preach. With all our eagerness there must be patience; with the widest possible charity there must still be refusal to compromise principles. The united Church must bring together all the elements of truth in all the several traditions, each unblunted as regards its definition and consequently as regards its cutting edge. But with that let us recognise that the drawing together of the elements of truth in the sundered traditions must also certainly involve modification in the expression of the truth that has been traditional and familiar. In a certain sense what is required is that every existing Christian communion should die in order to rise again into something more splendid than itself.

But that points to the action of God beyond all that men can ever do, and in the end the reunion of the Church will not be something fabricated by us at all; it will be the work of God resulting from a deeper devotion in all parts of the Church, and all members of all parts of the Church, to the One Lord of the Church. It is not through skill in negotiation, but through deeper devotion to the Lord Himself, that we may hope in the end to be brought into that full unity which corresponds to the Unity of God and His purpose for His people.

IV

"Go Forward"

A SERMON PREACHED IN ST. PAUL'S
ON SEPTEMBER 23RD 1943, AT THE INAUGURATION
OF THE BRITISH COUNCIL OF CHURCHES

> Wherefore criest thou unto me? Speak unto the children
> of Israel that they go forward.
>
> *Exodus* xiv. 15

IN 1937 between the two World Conferences at Oxford and
at Edinburgh a great service was held in this Cathedral
Church in which our prayers and praises were led by representatives of all the great Christian communions of the world
except the greatest of all. The preacher was my predecessor,
Archbishop Lord Lang, and he chose for his text the words
from the Book Exodus which I have chosen for mine to-day.
For our gathering here to-day inaugurates a new stage in
the enterprise to which he then pointed us. He urged that we
should continue to press forward in the search for the true
foundations on which the reunion of Christendom might be
accomplished; but he advised us not to wait for the achievement of that goal, but to go forward in united Christian witness and action on the basis of the unity which actually exists.

Since then the constitution of the World Council of
Churches has been approved by a great number of communions; joint action of the kind then urged upon us has been
increasingly undertaken; and to-day we inaugurate the Brit-

32

ish Council of Churches, the counterpart in our country of the World Council, combining in a single organisation the chief agencies of the inter-denominational co-operation which has marked the last five years.

In one sense this is more a matter of adjustment than of substantial innovation. Work hitherto conducted under three different agencies will now be conducted by one, the same people, for the most part, carrying on the various departments of the task. But in another sense it is a great event. Those departmental agencies, two of them hampered by very cumbrous names, could never catch the public imagination. The newly formed British Council of Churches may very likely do this, and so become the channel of new influences upon our common life.

There is no compromise of our distinctive principles in our coming together. But there is a choice involved between two different directions of attention, two different points of emphasis. In days when Christianity itself in its fundamental principles is unchallenged it may seem natural to lay most emphasis on the points which distinguish one communion from another. But in days like these when the basic principles of Christianity are widely challenged and in many quarters expressly repudiated, the primary need is for clear and united testimony to Christianity itself. The difference between Catholic and Protestant is very small as compared with the difference between Christian and non-Christian, between those who do and those who do not believe that in Jesus Christ God hath visited and redeemed His people.

Our differences remain; we shall not pretend that they are already resolved into unity or into harmony. But we take our stand on the common faith of Christendom, faith in God Creator, Redeemer and Sanctifier; and so standing together we invite men to share that faith and call on all to conform their lives to the principles derived from it.

As we co-operate with one another, so we shall be ready to welcome into co-operation with us in our particular enterprises all those who share the hope which inspires each enterprise, whether they share our basic faith or not. For there are many who wish to live by the principles which we claim as Christian who are as yet unable to accept the Christian faith in which we are persuaded that those principles are grounded. We shall need their help for the fulfilment of our hopes; and through their association with us we may lead them to the faith which as yet they have not found.

We owe united witness as a duty to our nation and to the hope of Christian civilisation. But we owe it still more to Our Lord Himself. While we shew ourselves to the world only as divided, we alienate men from Him. Only as we unite to present Him to men as the One Lord of life, our life and theirs, can we be true witnesses to Him. That is the conviction which above all else gives us courage and inspiration to-day.

"Speak unto the children of Israel that they go forward." The new opportunity is dawning—the opportunity for adventure in the Name of Christ, for uplifting Him as the Redeemer of social as of individual life. To us is given the high honour of sounding the call.

"Wherefore criest thou unto me?" If prayer be a substitute for action, then our choice must be for action. But indeed we must cry unto the Lord, not that He would do for us what He bids us do ourselves, but that He would uphold us as we go forward, sustaining our courage, and bracing our will for endurance. The promised land awaits us. Our Leader has trodden the way before us. He calls us to follow. By His enabling grace, we will.

V

Education for Peace

THE COMMEMORATION SERMON PREACHED AT OXFORD
ON SUNDAY, JUNE 21ST, 1942

> If ye abide in my word, then are ye truly my disciples;
> and ye shall know the truth and the truth shall make you
> free.
>
> *St. John* viii. 31

"THE truth shall make you free." He does not say "Through freedom ye shall find the truth", though the saying is sometimes quoted as if the latter were its real meaning.

The connection between truth and freedom is, no doubt, in the proper sense of the word dialectical; each, as it is progressively achieved, facilitates a further attainment of the other. If men's minds are held in bondage, there is no opportunity for them to advance in apprehension of truth; and it is only as they find truth that they become effectively free. The first of these two propositions is familiar and there is little need to labour the theme. The enquirer after truth must be unhampered by any consideration of pleasant or painful consequences of his conclusions or discoveries, if he is to acquire that sensitiveness to objective fact and perceptiveness of logical implications which are alike indispensable to the advance of knowledge. Upon this depends the vital importance of academic freedom, which in a British University there is no need to emphasise. This element in the dialectical tension between

35

truth and freedom is the special contribution of Hellenism to our civilisation. And it is impossible to prize it too highly.

Yet the other element is equally important, and to our generation, at any rate in this country, is less palatable. It is the special contribution of Judaism, and "salvation is from the Jews". Our Lord, in the much-quoted saying which I have taken as our text, lays down the principle with characteristic clearness and simplicity: "the truth shall make you free". Freedom, so far as it is of actual value, is not something native to men; we are not born free; we have to win freedom. Not only so—for we find that we cannot in fact win true freedom; we can only receive it. We do not make ourselves free; the truth, when we know it, makes us free.

For we set out upon the search for truth, as for other good things, full of bias and prejudice created by our self-interest and our passions. The disinterested love of truth is not natural to us, nor can we acquire it by an act of will in obedience to exhortation. In all mental activity there is selection, which must be guided by something. If, for example, a young man decides to devote his life to study in pursuit of truth, he cannot in fact study all aspects of reality at once. Shall he study the humanities or the exact sciences? No disinterested love of truth will help him here. Some inclination of his own temperament is likely to be the deciding factor. If he recognises this, no harm will be done; if not, he may be tempted to forget that there are other aspects of truth besides the one to which his own attention is given; and then he will press the application of his special interest as though there were no other.

Now let us suppose that he selects the exact sciences; he has again to choose the direction of his enquiries, for natural science is too vast a subject for any man to master in one lifetime. What shall guide him now? Very rarely it may happen that there is some obvious gap in the knowledge so far attained, and a purely intellectual interest can then prompt the desire to fill it. More commonly some other consideration is decisive. The Board of Faculty or a College needs a lecturer in a particular subject; or a commercial firm is concerned to promote research of a kind to improve its own technical processes. The scientific student must earn a living, and the direction of his study may often be settled by the openings available. Indeed such considerations generally carry him further than this; and the extent to which the course of scientific enquiry and consequent discoveries has been determined by economic causes is only now beginning to be adequately appreciated.

Now it may be possible, and perhaps not even difficult, to let the course of intellectual enquiry become entirely free from bias arising from the impulse which determined its direction, if the subject in question lies in the realm of the exact sciences. But to achieve such freedom from bias in the realms of psychology, of sociology, of history and of economics is very hard; and the first condition for overcoming the difficulty is to recognise its existence.

The difficulty does not concern the answer to questions that have been asked, but the need to ask questions from every angle of approach. When Professor Tawney was taking the earliest Tutorial Classes under the auspices of this University and the Workers' Educational Association he found that his working-class students asked questions about the manorial system and its modifications in the course of history to which the existing books gave no answer. He had to embark on extensive original research, of which the result was his book on *The Agrarian Revolution of the Sixteenth*

Century. The earlier historians were not dishonest; but their experience and that of their probable readers prompted some lines of enquiry, while that of the working-class students prompted others. The whole truth is found only when all possible lines of enquiry are followed and answers to all the questions are correctly given.

Freedom of enquiry, we may conclude, is never absolute. It is always conditioned by social pressures of one kind or another. Freedom is relative to its social and cultural context. Consequently it may be of great importance to control that context if the dangers arising from it are to be avoided.

At an earlier date, in the times of most of those benefactors whom we have commemorated to-day, the social and cultural context of this University was provided by Feudalism in its hey-day or its decay, and by the Church or its continuing influence when its period of dominance was past. All academic enquiry was conducted within a framework of accepted principles. In such circumstances the need is to insist on freedom and secure that it is as complete as possible.

Gradually, however, the unity has evaporated. A University was once a real totality of studies, each of which had its place in an intellectual economy of which the guiding principles were supplied by theology, the queen of sciences. Now it is a place where a multitude of studies are conducted with no relationship between them except those of simultaneity and juxtaposition. This may have been harmless, though not positively beneficial, at a time when the social and cultural context still supplied guiding principles. But that is no longer true. Alien systems of thought have captured large tracts of the continent of Europe; their influence has been not unknown amongst ourselves; our spiritual and intellectual heritage is in danger from these forces as truly as from the arms of our enemies; and we have to find the means of resisting them. To try to maintain an abstract freedom with no determinate goal is to court disaster. Freedom is not only freedom from something, but freedom for something. We need a determinate goal which will provide for us the directing principles which we seek.

The same need is apparent in our schools, especially the secondary schools, including those euphemistically described as "Public". Last week at Rugby we celebrated the centenary of Thomas Arnold's death. He owed his enormous effectiveness very largely to the definiteness of his educational ideal. His aim was to train Christian gentlemen. What similar definition of aim could to-day secure the assent of a majority of the Incorporated Association of Headmasters? We have learnt much since Arnold's time; indeed in one sense we have learnt too much, for we have extended the curriculum beyond all hope of integrating it in the service of a clearly conceived purpose. As a result of this the commercial motive has found an unrestricted field for its exercise, and many parents who keep their children at school beyond the age required by law do this with more concern for the larger income which the children may be enabled to earn than for the richer personality which they may be helped to develop.

We cannot go back to the goals and standards of a former generation. Can we find the goal which will give us our direction, our principles of action and our standards of success in the critical period through which our nation with all the rest of the world is passing? Greatly daring, I will offer one of which at least it may be said that it is consonant with the Christian interpretation of life and is relevant to the needs of the world in our time. For by common consent the first freedom to be won if any freedom is to be secure is freedom from war and from the threat of war. I urge therefore that our goal should be peace, and that we deliberately set ourselves to educate the coming generation for peace.

But if this is not to be misunderstood, two preliminary considerations must be faced. First, peace is not the normal condition of the world occasionally interrupted by war; war is the thing that happens of itself if no effective steps for its prevention are taken; peace needs to be made, and blessed are the peace-makers. Secondly, peace as a goal of educational or political effort must be conceived, not as a mere absence of fighting but as a positive and dynamic force. Peace in the negative sense may be an ignoble thing: it may be grounded in complacency or cowardice; it may be an acquiescence in evil. Peace as the goal of our striving, that peace the makers of which are blessed, must be nothing less than this: Goodwill effectively maintained against every form of greed.

Let us suppose such a goal to be accepted and see how it will affect our action. It will lead either to that form of pacifism which is ready to welcome pain and death, even of loved ones, rather than have recourse to the infliction of those, or else to the dedication of force to the maintenance of law between the nations as well as within them. Between those two I will not state the argument, but only record my own conviction that the latter, the subordination of force to law and to that end the endowing of law with force, is the more truly Christian way. But it will ask of us, and especially of the young men and women of the post-war period, great sacrifices. There must be no slipping back into the self-seeking and self-indulgence of the inter-war years. We must remain on a war footing that our assertion of goodwill against greed may be effective. And we must guard our hearts as against the devil from yielding to the temptation to use for our own greed the force which we maintain to uphold goodwill against greed of every kind.

Our moral training will have this end in view. It will call on young people to endure hardness as a discipline so that they may be ready to endure it in the service of true peace. Our science will be directed and utilised as a means to the promotion of fellowship, not primarily for rivalry, competition or the destruction of enemies.

Our study of literature, especially that of foreign countries, will be directed to the attainment of an understanding of them which may lead to a wise service of goodwill among them. Complaint has been made of late that our teaching of German literature has been based on the literary appreciation fashioned by our own culture rather than on a desire to understand German culture and its recent development. How far the complaint is justified only specialists can say; but if we take as our goal the peace which is the effective assertion of goodwill, our study of foreign literature must be such as helps us to estimate accurately the movements and forces with which we shall be confronted, as well as such as may cultivate our aesthetic sensibility.

It is, above all, in the teaching of history that such a goal will influence our course of action. In the presentation of history selection is inevitable. If the historian has no consciously accepted principle of selection, he will be guided by principles or influences to which he pays no attention, so that he cannot in any way check them or control them. If he adopts as his principle the relevance of various enterprises and movements to the attainment of peace as we have defined it, this will determine the perspectives and proportions of all his work. English historians throughout the nineteenth century selected and presented their material under the influence of the tacitly accepted hypothesis that the development of democratic self-government is progress. We have taught History on this principle in the schools of India, which accordingly asks of us the opportunity to make progress so understood. No doubt this hypothesis is sound, given certain conditions; but without those conditions it may be misleading. The only unconditional criterion of progress is that supplied by the Christian Gospel: God is Love, so that progress consists in the increasing preponderance of goodwill and love over self-interest and ill-will. That stands perennially. My suggestion is that the interpretation of this in terms of contemporary problems and needs gives us as our proximate goal that peace which is the effective assertion of goodwill against every kind of greed.

Above all, we must accept and impart the conviction that true freedom lives not in the atmosphere of claims and expectations but in that of duties and responsibilities. It was part of the achievement of the Middle Ages to associate privilege with duty; in an age when privilege is dwindling and equality increasingly takes its place, our need is to insist that freedom and responsibility go together. An attitude to life which expects and accepts benefits which have not been earned, whether in rich or in poor, is essentially servile in quality, and will lead to servility in the State however democratic its forms and machinery may be. There is, in the judgment of many of us, need that the State should take further steps towards establishing a basic economic and social security for all its citizens; but we must appreciate the temptations incidental to this, and use our educational influence to counteract them. If democracy is to live in the modern world, it will lay more emphasis on its duties than on rights.

Certainly this is necessary if democracy is to be the servant of peace as we have defined it. The effective assertion of goodwill against every form of greed involves, first, strong self-discipline, that the principle may be exemplified in the character of individuals; secondly, the acceptance of a general discipline of life, that greed in every department of life may be held in check; thirdly, a national discipline, whereby the nation itself in the persons of its citizens may be ready to supply force for the checking of greed among the nations while renouncing its use for the satisfaction of any greed of its own. We need to learn afresh that close association of freedom with discipline on which the moral teachers of mankind have always insisted, but against which the self-will of men has always rebelled.

Progress in this direction is possible only by a strong spiritual impulse. If such an aim is to be accepted by the nation, and by our Universities as the intellectual power-stations of the nation, the Christian members of nation and University must accept a great and exacting responsibility. They have so to represent in thought and life the principles of their faith that men find in it the integrating power which gives to all studies and activities their proper place and their delimitations. This is partly the work of theologians and pastors, but it is also the work of every Christian teacher, even, in his measure, of every Christian student. We cannot restore a predominance of Christian influence secured by statute; nor should we wish to restore it. For freedom is the first presupposition of the Gospel, and the Kingdom of God accepts no unwilling subjects. But if Christianity is true, we can win a predominance for Christian influence by shewing theoretically that the Gospel can restore the shattered unity of life, and by shewing practically its achievement of this for our own departments of activity.

If this is to be brought about, certain conditions must be

fulfilled. First, there must be a new and greater hazard of faith. Certainly we must be honest in thought and utterance, and not claim objective certainty where we have only subjective assurance. But let us avow that assurance where it exists; and let us seek to extend it by resolute experimentation with those parts of the Christian tradition of which as yet we may lack assurance. *Credo ut intelligam* must be our motto. Faith, intellectually regarded, begins as a hypothesis awaiting verification. The verification is found, if at all, only by experiment, the experiment of life. And for the most part those who make the experiment with thoroughness find the hypothesis verified, so that faith passes from the stage of dependence on authority to the stage of empirical assurance.

Secondly, we must be conscientious in our witness. May I suggest that the resident Fellow of a College who, being a professed Christian, is not frequent and regular in attendance at the daily service in his College chapel, is a fraudulent trustee for the treasure committed to him in his own faith? It makes a great difference to the boys and girls who come up from school whether or not they find the senior members of their College habitually joining together in the College worship. Upon this may largely turn the question whether or not the College is in appearance and effect a Christian College.

Thirdly, and as a prior condition without which these two can scarcely be made actual, Christian members of the University must be very sure that their allegiance to Christ comes before every other loyalty. The member of a College, senior or junior, must not think of himself, or lead others to think of him, as first and foremost a member of that College who happens, privately and incidentally, to be a Christian, but must think of himself, and by his conversation and conduct lead others to think of him, as first and foremost a Christian whose sphere of active discipleship is the College of which he is a member.

Those who put first their allegiance to Christ inevitably find themselves thereby united in fellowship with one another —the fellowship of the Holy Spirit. To a great extent this already exists in a living and effectual form. But we shall need the impact of a real body of believers upon the thought and work of the University if we are to recover for the Gospel in the new conditions and in this more Christian mode of pervasive influence, its former predominance and authority.

When I was first associated with the Student Christian Movement our friends from other centres used to describe the Christians of Oxford as living in a soft haze of mild conviction. Perhaps there is no ground for that reproach to-day. But in a world where new pagan systems of great definiteness and explosive force are battling for supremacy, convictions which are mild, soft or hazy will certainly not survive as influences on the world.

We are giving thanks to-day for those whose benefactions have enabled Oxford to play its great part through the centuries; as we commemorate them we cannot fail to notice that most of them were Christians who believed in Oxford as a Christian University. All Christian thanksgiving must take the form of dedication—that we may shew forth God's praise not only with our lips but in our lives. Let us dedicate ourselves to the great task of seeking truth, that the truth may make us free, in the service of the Prince of Peace.

VI

Our Trust and Our Task

BEING THE PRESIDENTIAL ADDRESS DELIVERED AT THE
ANNUAL MEETING OF THE NATIONAL SOCIETY
ON WEDNESDAY, JUNE 3RD, 1942

MY Friends,—I find myself delivering my first address as President of the National Society at a moment when, as we all know quite well, grave decisions will need before very long to be taken, because the educational system of the country is under review, and will, undoubtedly, in a greater or less measure, be re-shaped, and we must be ready to take our part fully and adequately in that process.

The National Society has found itself in the recent past somewhat hampered by its own form of organisation for the discharge of this responsibility, and, accordingly, it has been undertaking the reorganisation of its own machinery, in order that it may be in a better position for giving guidance to the Church, and, as we hope, also to the nation, in an emergency such as that which confronts us now. For this very reason it has not, at this moment, got a policy formally adopted to lay before the annual meeting of its members, and, through them, before the public. What is necessary for us at this moment is to review the situation and to consider afresh the principles upon which our whole work must be done. Happily, this is mainly a matter of reiterating what the Society has stood for from the beginning, though, perhaps, also finding a way in which this may be related to the whole situation in which we find ourselves. I propose, therefore, with your permission, to say something about the fundamental principles of all our work, and then to raise some questions concerning the ways in which we may best secure effectiveness for those principles in the situation with which we are dealing in our own time, and especially in the days immediately before us.

Now, first of all, I believe we are all agreed that the experiences through which the world has passed have impressed upon us more forcibly than ever before that all true education must be religious in its basis and texture. The question at issue in this war is fundamentally a religious question. It is the question whether the form of civilisation which has grown up out of the Christian doctrine about God and man is to have a wider scope in the affairs of men in the coming time, or whether, on the contrary, it is to be subject to very grave restrictions, and an added influence given to an outlook upon life which denies those fundamental doctrines of our religion, and which virtually puts the State of every nation, or, at any rate, of one nation, in the place of Almighty God. If we try to penetrate into the fundamental difference between the outlook of those peoples who now dominate Europe and the outlook that has been traditional among ourselves, and which is still the prevailing outlook of our people, we find it really does go back to those principles upon which you can affirm the dignity of human personality as we have known it, to the doctrine that man is a child of God, and that in his relationship to God he has a status independent of, and prior to, his membership of any earthly community. The freedom for which we are fighting is a freedom which has come down from those who believed that they ought to obey God rather than man, a freedom which is religious at its roots. This has very often been forgotten by the later exponents of the doctrine of liberty, but it is fundamental to any kind of liberty which is not to be the source of mere self-seeking in the individual and of chaos in society.

So more than ever the responsibility rests upon us to insist, not only that there shall be religious instruction as part of the whole curriculum in our schools, but that education is only adequate and worthy when it is itself religious. For the fact is that education must be in its effect, whatever the motive of those who organise and impart it, either religious or atheistic. There is no possibility of neutrality. To be neutral concerning God is the same thing as to ignore and deny Him. This is one of those questions to which the answer "No" is automatically given unless you deliberately give the answer "Yes"; to give no answer is to answer "No". If the children are brought up to have an understanding of life in which, in fact, there is no reference to God, you cannot correct the effect of that by speaking about God for a certain period of the day. Therefore our ideal for the children of our country is the ideal of a truly religious education.

Let us put the matter from another standpoint. It is the purpose of education to fit children for their life in the world so that they may conduct it in appropriate relation to their environment. There are three levels of environment. There is, undoubtedly, the sub-human environment: the world of physical nature. There is also the human world, the world of human relationships, and all that is included in the dealings of one man with another. No one disputes the fact that these two environments condition our life at every point, and no education can be adequate or worthy which does not fit people for dealing with both. But is there also a super-human environment? If there is, then it is certainly the most important of the three. If there is, then the relationship of the child to that which is above him, to God Himself, will determine in very large measure the mode of his activity in relation to the other two. To leave out this, or to treat it as optional, as a matter of private opinion, or something which is dependent upon individual temperament, is entirely to ignore the reality of the whole situation in which our work is to be conducted.

I am speaking of it in this way because I am persuaded that the primary need of our country is to recover a real philosophy of education. I asked a leading headmaster a little time ago what result would be obtained if you were to line up the members of the Incorporated Association of Headmasters, and moving along the line seek an answer to the question, "What are you aiming at with your boys? What do you want to produce?" And he said, "There is only one thing upon which any large number could possibly agree, and that would be the largest number of certificates and the highest possible number of credits." That is a rather satirical exaggeration. None the less I venture to suggest that a great deal of our difficulty in moving forward at the present time is that there is no general conception of what education really is. As Dr. Oldham has put it: We have learnt that the purpose of education is not the matter taught, but the person who has to learn it. We are concerned with teaching persons rather than subject matter, but we have at the same time apparently ruled out of court all enquiry concerning the nature and destiny of personality. We are concerned in training people: we never ask what kind of thing people ought to be. That is a hopeless position. Dr. Arnold knew perfectly well what he was aiming at: and we have learned a great deal in many departments of education in the hundred years since he died. (We celebrate the centenary of his death on Saturday week.) We have learned a great deal about the technique of education. We have learned so much, indeed, of the technique of it, that we are in danger of forgetting the purpose of it. Though we should certainly not be able to obtain general agreement on his aims concerning education, it is, surely, of the utmost consequence that we should recover, and, if possible, secure general assent—it would hardly be universal—for a fundamental conception with regard to the real purpose of education. These are questions that should arise from time to time out of our changing circumstances, and which should find their appropriate answers.

Now there is hope that something of this kind is possible to-day, mainly for two reasons. There is, undoubtedly, a growing public concern, both about education and about the religious quality of education. Certainly there is about education as a whole. Large sections of the nation are becoming deeply concerned who, until lately, have paid very little attention to it. That is partly due to motives more commercial than strictly educational; but it is a fact of which some advantage can be taken. Along with that is a very widespread sense of need, and the consciousness of a gap which needs to be filled, and which *we* know can only be filled by religious faith. It is not true to say that there is as yet any great measure of agreement that it is that which alone can fill the gap, but there is a growing consciousness of that empty space which must be filled if we are to have a sense of direction, and of power to follow it.

In the past the main instrument of the Church in upholding its principles has been the Church School. At first there was no other instrument for the purpose at all. Let us remember always, partly in order that we may claim for the Church the credit due to it, and partly also as a guide to our own thinking, that in the period in which the Church began establishing Schools, the State was not doing it. Other religious bodies were also taking an active part. But education was provided entirely through voluntary agencies, and until 1870 the activity of the State in that field was very small. The tentative quality of its approach is always vivid to my mind because of my father's experience. He was appointed Principal of the first Training College there ever was. It was at Kneller Hall, now a place for training bandmasters. The teachers whom my father was to train were going to teach in the new institutions erected under the new Poor Law of 1834. But when he had trained the teachers there were no schools for them to teach in; and that Training College came to an end because the teachers when trained could not exercise their profession. The approach of the State to the matter has been rather hesitant and tentative! In 1870, however, it took it up in good earnest, and from that time onward the part played by the State in the field of education has been steadily developing. Nor is there any possibility that it can be hindered, and I do not suppose that any of us wish to hinder it. What we are concerned about is that we should continue to uphold in any system now mainly administered by the State, those principles, those elements of supreme value, which were characteristic of the Church Schools, and were the chief aim for which they were planned.

In that early period when the Church was itself the founder of the Schools, there were various tendencies that, to some extent, have created a prejudice against us. There was, for example, the very natural tendency for the incumbent to regard the schoolmaster as part of his parochial staff, and to hold that he was there apparently to carry on one particular department of the Church's work. That is what he was there for. The Church had founded the School; it maintained it; it found the stipend of the teacher; and, of course, the teacher was, therefore, part of the staff of the parish. That is a state of things that cannot continue, when the State itself has become the main source of the educational supply, and there is a great teaching profession spread far beyond the Church Schools. But there are some areas which have never been adjusted to the new situation; thus there has grown up an unhappy prejudice in the minds of the teachers leading them to suppose that their position in Church Schools is one of less dignity than in other schools. Now that is quite disastrous. I know everyone in this hall will agree with me when I say we must take the utmost pains to secure that there is no ground for that suspicion; that the status of a teacher in the Church School is every bit as dignified and independent as in any other school; though, of course, he is appointed to carry out certain specified aims which are therefore part of his duty.

Along with the increase in the activity of the State has gone the growth of professional feeling among teachers. This, again, is not only all to the good, but is something quite indispensable to education. It is of the most vital importance that the whole body of the teachers should feel themselves to be a responsible and honourable part of the public service, and we must not desire, upon our part, anything that can hinder the growth of such a sense among them; for in all walks of life professional honour is a main safeguard against tendencies of any kind to slackness or neglect.

Further, there has been a very great development in the growth of the efficiency of educational administration. With the growth of variety of the type of schools, which we all recognise to be necessary, especially in the later stages, the central administration becomes more and more important. Dr. Mansbridge this morning was urging upon us that a very much larger part, at any rate of later education, ought to be through manual activity. There are a great many children whose brains are better developed by setting their fingers to work than by calling upon them to read books. The number of children who can absorb freely out of the printed page is really limited. The very same ideas, to a large extent, can be imparted by setting children to do things, and when what they attempt to do goes wrong, to find out the reason why. The best way for very many boys, at any rate, to learn mathematics is for them to do constructive work: the necessary training must then be given in order that they may be able to carry through the work entrusted to them. But, amid all this variety, if boys and girls are to have the opportunity of obtaining the sort of education that will really fit them for their work in life, then there must be great development of central organisation and planning. So you get built up the whole civil service of education which has conferred such great benefits upon the nation, and which inevitably regards the field from the point of view of administrative efficiency.

Well, it is in that situation that we find our tradition in many ways challenged from without; and if we are to meet that challenge we must do it much more thoroughly than merely by saying "We believe in the dual system", or "We believe in Church Schools". We must say what it is about the dual system that we believe in: and why the thing we believe in can be secured by the dual system and in no other way. We must say what it is about Church Schools that we believe in, and to what extent it is true that that can be secured by Church Schools and in no other way.

I would very daringly suggest that one value of the dual system is its duality. I wish to suggest that there is a very great advantage in the educational field in maintaining real variety of type, with a considerable measure of individual liberty and autonomy. Many of the non-provided schools represent that element in our system at the present time, and we want to find a way of retaining, quite apart from all religious interest in the matter—of retaining, and, if it may be, of extending this element of freedom and autonomy in the individual schools. I do not think our administration desires mechanical uniformity; but there is an inherent and inevitable tendency in any bureaucratic control towards mechanical uniformity; with the best will in the world the administration cannot prevent it increasing. In face of what has been happening in Europe, the importance of regaining the real independence of the several schools ought, surely, to be obvious to all of us. If we wish to avoid totalitarianism, there is a merit in the very duality of the dual system. I should not in the least mind it becoming a triplicity; but I should regret it becoming a mere unity. There is no doubt, for example, that the Church Schools are able, as a general rule, to give more sense of corporate unity to the school, to create a stronger sense of corporate life, to bring into the Schools elements of special and outstanding interest, often of a quite inspiring type, which is far more difficult for schools administered under public authority. The managers appeal to friends who may come in on special occasions in the life of the School, lending a touch of special individuality to it in a way that would hardly be possible otherwise. Moreover, when the children reach the age for leaving school, they do not feel that they have gone out of that building for ever, for the building goes on, and is used for many functions in which they take a part.

There is a bridge between the school and the wider life outside, which is very hard to produce where there is no society besides the State to which the school belongs.

Those are general educational considerations, not, I suppose, of the first importance, but, I believe, of very real importance, if we are to avoid the mechanising of the whole scheme.

Now we turn to the Church School itself, and the points on which stress has been laid in our defence of the Church School. Have circumstances in any way changed so that at one point or another we could secure what we are standing for with some real modifications of the system? I think the main points have been three. One is, the content of the teaching itself, the syllabus, or Church Catechism; the second is, the appointment of the teachers; the third is, the living association between the School and the Church.

As regards the content of the teaching, I think it is true that we have less occasion for anxiety than was the case formerly. There is a great growth in agreement between ourselves and the spokesmen of the Free Churches concerning what should be taught to the children in the Schools. A great many of the Agreed Syllabuses are quite admirable. Some of them may leave a good deal still to be desired; but the existence of the really good syllabuses is a factor of which we ought to take notice in the case of the provided schools, and which we are bound to consider in relation to our own Schools if we are to present our case in such a way that others will pay attention to it. Therefore I leave that for the moment merely as a question: Is it a fact that there are changes in the whole situation which might make it possible for us, without the surrender of anything of the highest value, to agree to some modification, some accommodation, in so far as our concern for Church Schools has been directed to the content of the teaching given?

Secondly, the appointment of the teachers. This has been the best way, if not at times the only way, of securing that the teachers shall be such as are really qualified to give the teaching which is required under the Trust Deed, and which we are pledged to maintain. Has anything happened which makes a difference concerning that? Well, there are proposed changes in the training of teachers which would, if they take effect in course of time, lead to a very much larger number of really competent and equipped teachers. I think there is a growing sense in the teaching profession itself about the vital importance of religious teaching in the Schools. I do not think that process has, as yet, gone very far. Improvement now made in training could not produce its full effect for some fifteen or twenty years, but we should take note of it as an element which gives us hope, and might give us an occasion for being ready to modify our outlook. At this point we are bound to say that that situation has not arisen on any large scale as yet. But the influence of the "refresher courses" now widely given is an increasingly important factor.

Thirdly, the living association between the School and the Church. I do not see how that is to be provided in any way at all except through the maintenance of a body of managers constituted substantially as the managers are constituted now. Through the body of managers, if they really play their part, and through the parish priest playing his special part, there is established a living connection between the School and the Church which I regard as of fundamental and vital importance and value, and which is really quite independent of the use of any particular syllabus. When we remember how psychology is teaching us that suggestion is a much more vital force than instruction, I think we shall see that the presence of the clergyman, and other people known to be active Church members, in and about the School, and taking care of it, has great influence in the lives of the children, and is more important than the use of some particular form of instruction.

That is the way in which we ought to be approaching this matter—trying to analyse our tradition, so as to get clear in our own minds, and to set before other people, what are the points in our tradition which have led us to stand for it so firmly and to safeguard our trust, and to see how far in the changed circumstances the old method is the best way of serving this end. I am not going at the moment to give an answer to that question. This is one of the things I hope the National Society is going to look into, so that it may present a reasoned statement, with which we can go to the Authority in the State with every reason for anticipating that they will meet us fairly when we present the matter in a form that they can appreciate. It must be in that kind of way that we do it, rather than by repeating the old phraseology, about which they have become very suspicious.

I regard as a most hopeful sign in the whole situation—the astonishing approximation which has been growing among the theologians of all Christian Communions. Now if that tendency is allowed a little time to develop, we shall find ourselves in a world where the great body of the Christian Communions in this country is really able to stand together, and I am sure that we should encourage in every possible way all that can be done to that end. One of the things which we must do to-day, without the surrender of principles or of our trust, is the removal of whatever may hinder the growth of this agreement.

I have already spoken about the attitude of the teachers to

our whole tradition. A large number of the Schools are, as a matter of fact, in the hands of one denomination; a large proportion of the posts in which men might be first tried out in positions of leadership are thus closed to all who are not of that denomination. It is that, rather than the question of tests for teachers in its old form, which seems to be an infringement of professional freedom and dignity. How far we can meet that, I do not know. But let us understand what is in their mind, and recognise that there is a genuine difficulty from the point of view of teachers who, it may be, are quite religious men, but are not members of the Church of England. Let us appreciate it in order that as we put our case to them and claim that the interest of the children must come first, we may be able to claim from them the same kind of sympathy for our tradition.

As regards the Free Churchmen, we must recognise that the point at which they feel grievance is that of the single school area. We must consider how far there is the possibility, again without the surrender of principle or trust, so to arrange the teaching in those schools as, at least, to diminish the grievance which they feel. I have been assured by a leading Free Churchman that if we could remove this sense of grievance and injustice, resulting from the control of the Church in single school areas, we should almost remove the Free Church objection to the dual system or to Church Schools. That is probably an over-statement. But I am bound to say that I think a devoted Methodist, or Baptist, resident in a parish where there is only one school, and that a Church of England School, has some ground for complaint in the position in which he finds himself, for he must send the child to that school. Even though provision may be offered for Free Churchmen to give instruction in the principles of their denomination—which this Society has always urged should be done—they very often are quite unable to take advantage of it, so that the offer seems rather an empty gesture in the eyes of the Free Churchmen. These are areas in which we could investigate afresh how far the values, for the sake of which we have maintained Church Schools, values which we insist shall be maintained in the days to come, can be preserved, with modifications for meeting the grievances felt outside. Along with that there must be perfect clearness in our minds that we could not consent to any general abolition of the dual system; we should have to fight against that.

Now it has been thought in some quarters that if the five points which were urged by the Archbishops some eighteen months ago were conceded—I do not like the word "conceded", but suppose those five points were—to use that horrid word—implemented—it would be reasonable to modify very profoundly the dual system. We might take up the question as to how far we might agree to modify the dual system on that ground, and we should, I hope, be perfectly reasonable in that matter. But we cannot recognise the fact that something that is put forward on behalf of general religious education itself constitutes a reason for modifying the dual system. It must be gone into on its own merits. The five points were put forward for improving religious instruction in provided schools on the basis of an explicit assumption that Church Schools would remain. The two cannot be balanced, one against another. But in so far as we can be satisfied with the religious teaching in provided schools our case for maintaining the dual system unmodified is, of course, affected.

Secondly, there is a proposal in some quarters for a national syllabus of religious instruction, and an article appeared in *The Times Educational Supplement* asking that the Archbishops' desire for a national syllabus may be acted upon. But the Archbishops have expressed no such desire. My predecessor has told me that he certainly does not welcome it. I certainly do not welcome it. And I have no reason to think that the Archbishop of York welcomes it. What there might be, I think, with some advantage is a general understanding of the ground which should be covered, so that the teacher who is adequately trained in teaching in one area would find that his training was equally effective when he moved to another area, and that he was not suddenly left with a great deal of new matter to master. There might be a kind of common skeleton on which each syllabus could be formed. But I should be opposed at this stage to an attempt to frame a national syllabus, first, because the only chance of getting one would be by reducing its content to a degree which would be disastrous, and, secondly, because if you adopted a syllabus on a national scale you would have extreme difficulty in modifying it if ever you wanted to do so. We know what has happened in the past. One Local Authority has learned from another. An Authority which feels that its own syllabus is out of date collects the syllabuses of other Authorities and studies them, and makes another one, imitating the others where they have proved successful and avoiding the points found to be defective. So the Authority with the old-fashioned syllabus suddenly leaps into the van with the best of all. There has been in the past an amazing development of this, the syllabus of one Authority being of use to another Authority, and in that way progress has been possible. Once you had a national syllabus, I am afraid any further progress in the matter of the syllabus itself would be very difficult, so difficult as to be almost impossible.

Thirdly, we could not agree to anything that constituted

the wholesale transfer or surrender of our Church Schools. We are prepared to survey the field, to see how those things for which we have stood may best be served in the modern conditions: we are prepared to consider this, that or the other specific modification of the system we have inherited, but anything like wholesale surrender or transfer of our Church Schools we should have to resist.

I hope we shall go forward quite determined about our basic principles, but in a quite reasonable frame of mind, in the conviction that, if we can instil into the whole situation, not only the firmness of faith, but also the conciliatory influence of a reasonable disposition, we may without bitter struggle secure for the children of our country an increasingly effective Christian religious education.

VII

Fellowship in War

AN ADDRESS DELIVERED AT THE SERVICE OF INTERCESSION
FOR CHINA IN ST. PAUL'S CATHEDRAL
ON WEDNESDAY, JULY 8TH, 1942

In righteousness he doth judge and make war.
Revelation xix. 11

THAT is a description of the Word of God who is King of Kings and Lord of Lords. The Word of God is not a passive principle of rational unity but an active force of moral judgment. The unity of all things which philosophers rightly seek is not something which already exists, waiting to be discovered by us, it is something which is being fashioned by toil and strife, by agony and bloody sweat; the Word of God is the Captain of that enterprise and He calls us to be His fellow workers.

In that supreme undertaking we are now working out a critical stage. This world conflict is a turning point not only of man's age-long endeavour to achieve a true civilisation, but of the purpose of God as it is displayed in human history. Great principles are at stake; great spiritual forces are engaged. We ought to recognise more fully than we commonly do the spiritual nature of the conflict and our need of spiritual resources if we are to secure the triumph of the cause we serve.

Our gathering here to-day should represent a recognition

of this truth. We come here as children of our Father in heaven to confess before Him that in His will alone is our true peace, that only by serving Him can we be truly free, and that only in the strength He gives can we serve Him effectively. We must not come to Him to ask that He will do our wills; we may only come to Him to be made worthy and able to do His. But we believe with all our hearts that as we strive our utmost in the conflict which engulfs the world we are without doubt serving His purpose, and with full confidence we seek His guidance and His aid.

Among the united nations pledged to the cause of freedom, China is, so to speak, the senior partner. It is not yet three years since war broke out in Europe; for five years its horrors have been familiar in China. She was the victim of the first in the long series of lawless and criminal aggressions which were the prelude to the world-wide war. Her suffering has lasted longer and has been more intense than our own. Her endurance has been such as to inspire all who are now associated with her in defence of freedom and international order.

To all who know her history China is an object of veneration. She had achieved a civilisation of high order when our ancestors were wild barbarians. She has learnt the secret of partnership with nature and fellowship among men as hardly any other people under heaven has learnt it. In her tradition of reverence for former members of each family she supplies to each growing generation a sense of partnership with those who have gone before and with those who shall come after which is among the surest of all foundations for social stability. Her outstanding virtues of constancy, honesty and patience render her immune to many of the shocks that have shattered other societies. She has maintained in her long isolation from the world a peaceful dignity and unruffled wisdom which rebuke our restless avarice and our hasty superficialities. The great art of China has for centuries offered the most revealing symbols of the calm of eternity which human genius has contrived. Before that age-long culture—so sure in its foundations, so pervasive in its influence—we offer the homage of heart-felt veneration.

Now for a hundred years the outside world has been pressing upon China; there are episodes upon which we look back with shame for our own conduct in them. And since the beginning of the twentieth century China has been forced against her will to take note of the modern movements among men. There has been some turmoil of thought and action. But the main impression created is that of a national spirit serene in its strength of purpose rising above one crisis after another in fulfilment of a destiny continuous with that noble past.

But no former crisis has been so searching as that of the last six years. Yet now more than ever, under the great leadership of her noble Generalissimo, we see her calm and collected in spirit, holding her own with far inferior equipment against the onslaught of an enemy who had long prepared for the acts of banditry by which the civilised world has been outraged. How has China met this challenge? Has she concentrated all attention on the destruction of the foe, indifferent to the effect of this on her own national life? On the contrary, in face of war and under its stimulus she has set about the organisation of a veritable renaissance in education and in the planning of her social life. Such a spirit is unconquerable. Through whatever sacrifices she may have to pass, China will stand when the war is over, a mighty people strengthened by this period of national discipline, accepting what she finds acceptable in the traditions of Europe and

America—individualist and communist alike—and subordinating these to the spirit of her own perennial culture.

Such is the people with whom we are proud to be associated to-day; such is the people to whom we pledge our utmost co-operation in the common cause; such is the people for whose deliverance from invasion, oppression and cruel warfare we are gathered here to pray. They and we have much in common; on the basis of what is common to our traditions we can make fruitful to both nations the diversities which are there in equal measure. But first we stand together to bear what must be borne, to strike as opportunity is given, to persevere till victory crowns our effort and opens the way to co-operation in the tasks and acts of peace.

We recall the extent to which the Christian faith has influenced the renaissance of China. In 1912 Dr. Sun Yat Sen, the first President of the Chinese Republic and a Christian, took the unprecedented step of appealing to all Christian people for their prayers on behalf of the new Republic. The Generalissimo and his wife are Christians who begin each day with prayer. We join our prayers with theirs. Around this Cathedral in which we are met is an area devastated by air raids. In the Chinese capital, still more grievously damaged, Chinese Anglicans have bought a site in the heart of the ruins and have set up there a church of matting and straw to be replaced after the war by a permanent building. It is dedicated to the unknown heroes—the police, the telephone-linesmen, the road-menders, the mothers of children, who have given their lives in constancy to duty during air raids. In another city four times besieged, once burnt, continually bombed, a service was conducted once a month in English for Europeans; and the collection taken at the first service was sent to the Dean of St. Paul's for a bombed parish in the City of London.

It is right to recall also that from almost every engagement or occupied city comes the record of Japanese Christians who showed gentleness and sympathy where all else was bitter.

At this time, when China enters on the sixth year of war, we are asked to give with all the generosity of which we are capable to the Aid to China Fund. Among the claims of these exacting days this surely takes a foremost place. When we think of China's past tradition, of the contribution which it is in her power to make to the world in future generations, of her long struggle and agony, and of the bond that unites her cause with ours, we must open our hearts and our purses to her appeal. As we stand together in effort and devotion, so let our partnership be manifest in the generosity of our gifts.

Upon such a partnership we invoke the blessing of God. For we have no doubt that in spite of our unworthiness to serve it the cause committed to us is His cause and all we do for it can be made an offering to Him, who in righteousness doth judge and make war.

VIII

The Church's Approach to the Problem of Venereal Disease

AN ADDRESS DELIVERED TO A CONFERENCE CONVENED BY
THE CENTRAL COUNCIL FOR HEALTH EDUCATION
ON FRIDAY, FEBRUARY 26TH, 1943

THE problem with which we are concerned is obviously in part a medical problem; but it is also a social, moral and spiritual problem. Consequently there should be the utmost possible co-operation between all the various forces and organisations concerned for the welfare of the people—spiritual, moral, social and medical. For this reason I greatly welcome the opportunity which has been given to me of taking part in this Conference.

Before I go further I must make clear certain points with regard to my own position. Early in last autumn the Minister of Health wrote me a most kind letter inviting me to accept the Presidency of the Central Council for Health Education. I made some enquiries, as a result of which I felt able to accept the invitation, and did so. I was aware that one of the most immediate concerns of the Council would be educational propaganda with regard to venereal disease, and I hoped that I could take some useful part in this. The need was evident and urgent, and I had ascertained that there was sufficient agreement of outlook between myself and the Executive Committee. I wished, as I still wish, to press for a rapid extension of the provision of clinics and a great development of public propaganda; and in the latter I wished to secure that the moral appeal should take a foremost place.

Then Regulation 33B appeared. I was greatly disquieted, but decided to await the debates and decisions of Parliament. These were such as to make some declaration from me imperative. I at once wrote to the Minister submitting my resignation of the Presidency of the Council, saying that I could not hold that office and keep silent, while at the same time it seemed unfair to him to use as a vantage-ground for criticising his Regulation a post which he had honoured me by inviting me to fill. After a good deal of consultation the Minister most generously asked me to retain the office of President while being free also to criticise the Regulation. So much I have felt obliged to say by way of introduction, because otherwise it might be thought that I was taking a wrongful advantage of my position here.

I do not in the least want to divert attention from the main theme to a discussion of the merits or demerits of Regulation 33B. My references to it will be incidental and illustrative of my main point. This is, that where spiritual, moral, social and medical aspects are all discoverable in one fact or tendency, they should receive attention in that order; or, to put it concretely, inasmuch as the problem before us is both moral and physical, the moral element in it is the more important and should have the first attention.

Now it is a certainty that venereal disease is communicated almost—not quite, but almost—entirely in illicit sexual intercourse. In other words, if men and women would abstain from fornication, the problem confronting the Minister of Health would be reduced to negligible proportions. What was left would be a purely medical problem; but only that minute residuum is a purely medical problem. The great bulk of the evil is primarily a moral problem.

Therefore it ought to be approached in the first instance in the way most likely to produce the desired moral results. The object first to be aimed at is the practice of continence. What are the influences which may be expected to lead to this? If we are thinking of a long-term policy, it is plain that the influence of a good home vastly exceeds any other. All that we can do to promote healthy family life, both by adequate supply of housing and by help to parents in the wise upbringing of their children, is of inestimable value. Next will come the teaching and influence of school, and of such young people's associations as help to form character during adolescence. But far more potent than any teaching, any exhortation, any attempted compulsion, is the suggestion afforded by habits of practice and conversation and by the attitude adopted by authority.

It really is time that this elementary psychological principle should be universally accepted and acted upon: if teaching and suggestion are in conflict, suggestion will win every time. Therefore the first question we have to ask about any proposed action in this field is "What suggestion is it offering?"—not "What result does it aim at?" nor "What inducements or penalties does it provide?" but "What suggestion will it make?"

It is a fundamental principle of far-reaching importance that Governments affect the conduct of their subjects far more by the principles implicit in their acts than by the requirements of legislation or the severity of the penalties attached to neglect of those requirements. Thus the earlier attempts to put down crimes of violence and various kinds of theft by means of savage punishment were a total failure. The callousness in inflicting pain, or the readiness to take life, displayed by the Government encouraged these bad qualities in its subjects more than the penalties restrained them. To bring this home to the legislators of his generation was one of the great achievements of Jeremy Bentham.

In dealing with venereal disease our rulers systematically ignore this principle. Thus in the Army, with a view to checking venereal disease, instruction is given to recruits in the use of prophylactics. The implication and suggestion is that the authorities expect a considerable number to practise fornication. There is no doubt at all in my own mind—though proof is evidently impossible—that this method, by its inevitable suggestion, causes an increase of promiscuous intercourse, and therefore also an increase of the disease which it is designed to prevent. And the root trouble is the treatment of what is primarily a moral problem as if it were primarily a medical problem.

The fundamental objection to Regulation 33B is the same. There is much else about it which I dislike, but I confine myself to this main point. Its very existence tends to create the suggestion that infectious "contacts" are being dealt with and that the concern of the Government is to make fornication medically safe. Thus here too the fundamental error is allowed to determine policy: what is primarily a moral problem with a medical aspect is being treated as if it were primarily a medical problem with a moral aspect. The harm is all the greater because this Regulation stands alone; if it had been introduced after a vigorous educational campaign had been launched it would have taken its place in a different perspective and its evil suggestion would have been far less potent.

We have now to redress the balance as far as we may by the educational effort of which this Conference is a part.

Before I pass on to that, I must ask leave to add one word about the proposal advanced by some critics of the Regulation, namely that we should go still further and make venereal disease compulsorily notifiable. That would be far worse than the Regulation. There is enough moral sensitiveness left among us to make the contraction of these diseases a matter of shame. If any man or woman who was known to be infected were thereupon to be isolated, the great majority would conceal the early symptoms, and the number seeking early treatment would be greatly reduced; thus the chief means of checking the disease would be removed. The only way in which this could be averted would be by obliterating the sense of shame still attaching to what is taken as evidence of misconduct, and that would be worse both morally and medically.

But there is a great evil and a grave menace to be met. How does the Church approach it? And here let me, on behalf of the Church, so far as I may, publicly acknowledge a great sin of omission. If we criticise the Government for tackling the matter in what we think the wrong way, we must acknowledge our own failure hitherto to tackle it in the right way. We have done something through our Moral Welfare Councils and other channels; but we have not given the public teaching that is needed. We have shared with others the cowardly tendency to avoid the subject because it is so disagreeable.

First, then, in our educational campaign must be put the sacredness of sex. The sexual function of men and women is primarily that whereby they co-operate with God in the creation of His children; that is why they are said to procreate—to act on behalf of the Creator. Plainly such a function calls for reverence in action and in speech. No treatment of the subject can be satisfactory which ignores or obscures this fundamental truth.

Secondly, the duty and the possibility of chastity must be made clear. There is an immense amount of sheer ignorance and error to be dispelled at this point.

These two positive points need all possible emphasis, and should be regarded by all concerned in the enterprise as fundamental.

Thirdly, ample provision should be made, both in the forces and in civilian life, for abundance of wholesome educational and recreational activity. One main occasion of misconduct is boredom and monotony of life. All good club organisation for adolescents and young adults is a real contribution to purity of life. Especially should there be facilities for happy social intercourse between men and women, in dances and otherwise. This is of particular importance for men and women in the Forces, who are inevitably separated from their homes and families.

Fourthly, inducements to indulge in alcoholic drinks should be removed as far as possible. I have heard of dances and other entertainments arranged for men and women of the Forces where none but alcoholic drinks have been in evidence; that seems to me little short of criminal. It is, of course, notorious that a very large proportion of those who misbehave do so under the influence of alcohol.

Fifthly, instruction should be given widely (*a*) in the dangers inseparable from promiscuity and (*b*) in the duty of seeking early treatment if there is the smallest ground for suspecting that infection has been contracted.

Sixthly, to facilitate this early treatment, clinics should be provided as rapidly as possible, so placed that one is within easy reach of every town or village in the country. The very slow expansion of the provision of clinics after the outbreak of war is a serious blot on our record of administrative efficiency.

Seventhly, so far as disciplinary action is called for, let it be administered with the suggestion of indignation that any man should have so behaved as to risk the infection. This is not impracticable. If I am rightly informed, one of the best records for immunity from venereal disease held by any unit of our Forces in the last war was that of a Canadian regiment in which no prophylactics were issued nor instruction in the use of them given, but ablution centres were provided, any man who thought he might have become infected was expected to make use of these, and actually to contract the disease was treated as a serious military offence.

At least that represents the right order of approach. Human nature is frail; any yielding to this temptation involves consequences so serious to military efficiency and to social and physical welfare that it is right to provide the means of checking those consequences and to expect that they shall be used. What is quite deadly is to give the impression that misconduct is accepted as normal or that the chief interest of authority is to enable people to do wrong with impunity. We are not called upon to deceive ourselves or to suppose that misconduct is very uncommon; but for the sake of society as a whole, for the sake of the waverer who is as yet innocent, and for the sake of the man or woman who has actually indulged, let all our handling of this topic express the conviction that fornication, be it rare or common, is something that arouses the condemnation of all decent citizens and "the dreadful astonishment of God".

IX

A Call to Men

AN ADDRESS DELIVERED TO THE CHURCH OF ENGLAND
MEN'S SOCIETY ON JULY 10TH, 1943

WE are here to make a call to the men of our Church. Let us ask ourselves frankly whether men as a whole do their duty by the Church—its worship and its activities—as women do, or (which alone is really important) as Our Lord requires of them. And let us face this question in full view of the opportunity and challenge of this hour.

Everyone is planning the good world we hope to see when the war is over. These plans all concern the machinery of life. It is vitally important to get it into good order, but that will not by itself give us the good world. Far more important is the outlook and moral quality of the men and women who are to work the social machinery of that time, whether new or old. There will be some new factors added to the present situation, and I will mention them very briefly. We shall all be extremely tired, and weariness is a selfish condition, because when we are tired we try to avoid effort, and it always takes an effort to see how the world is affecting other people, while we know how it affects ourselves without making any effort at all. So we must expect, unless we successfully guard against it, a great access of selfishness, in the individual, family, class and nation. Along with this there will be a mood of relaxation in reaction from the restraints and discipline of war-time. And these will be factors complicating a situation already complicated enough.

When we survey the moral situation of the country to-day, we find two apparently contradictory features in it. On the one side there is the picture of splendid endurance, mutual helpfulness and constancy which during the "blitz" reached heroic proportions, but is still present in the even more testing time in which A.R.P. workers, Civil Defence units and the like are waiting for what may happen but either does not happen at all or happens on a very small scale. In these respects the morale of the country is magnificent.

Over against that is a really alarming collapse in respect of honesty and sex morality. I think that what has happened is this: It is always true that the actual moral customs of a people depend on and are bound up with the social structure of their life; that is why different kinds of conduct are judged right or wrong in different parts of the world or at different times, while the principles of right and wrong remain unchanged. Any breaking of the structure of life always weakens a morality which mainly depends on convention. Convention is not to be despised; it is the deposit of the experience of the community in which it is found, accumulated through many generations; but it depends upon the social context in which it arises. When that is greatly altered, especially if it is altered suddenly, whatever is conventional and no more will collapse. Our moral behaviour was largely regulated by conventions down to the last war, which administered a considerable shock to our traditional social structure, and with that shock the conventions were greatly shaken. But that was nothing to the shock which this war has administered; people have been taken from their families, the family itself has been largely disintegrated, men and women are brought together in wholly artificial aggregations which are known to be temporary. In such conditions the old conventions lose their power unless there is something else behind them. Before the war our chief moral enemy was listlessness and purposelessness: people had nothing definite to live for which gave them a goal for their endeavours and put a restraint upon their impulses. The war has corrected that and has given a purpose to life at any rate till it is over, and it is in service of that purpose that the fine moral quality of our people has shewn itself. But it is not a purpose which at all evidently covers the whole of life; and where people do not see a direct connection between a familiar moral requirement and the war purpose, the old conventions fail and nothing takes their place. People are not conscious of injuring the war effort by dishonesty or by sexual indulgence, and as the war effort is the one regulating factor in their lives, these parts of their lives remain unregulated. That at any rate is how I read our situation.

If I am right, the evil in it can only be cured by a return to first principles. I am sure that it is one of our primary duties at present to be talking quite constantly about the evil of the prevailing dishonesty and untruthfulness. In what does that evil consist? I wonder how many of you could mention on demand the reason which St. Paul gives for telling the truth? It is that "we are members one of another". For that belonging to one another can only exist when there is mutual confidence: the supreme evil of any lie and of any act of dishonesty is that it does something to weaken that mutual confidence. Also it is a failure to recognise the personal quality of the person to whom the lie is told or who is cheated, and these two things—respect for personality and mutual trust —are the very heart of that free civilisation which we are fighting to defend. It is always true that great things are achieved or maintained by individual contributions, each of which in itself is negligible. If you were to withdraw the individual contribution to the war effort of any single citizen, except perhaps the Prime Minister, no one would know the difference; ye victory is only possible if everyone of us plays his part. People can see it in that connection, but it is just as true about the whole fabric of a free civilisation; it can only be established and it can only be maintained if people will live and govern their conduct in accordance with the principles of respect for one another's personality and mutual trust and confidence. Every lie, every bit of cheating, tends to undermine that and is treachery to our cause.

It is just the same with sex relationships. To use that function of our nature as an opportunity of passing amusement always involves treating another person as a plaything or a toy. That is destructive of the freedom we are fighting to maintain, for the heart of that freedom is the dignity of personality. But here, even more than in the other case, the religious background makes all the difference in the world. There is nothing nasty about sex as God has made it; there is no reason why it should not be spoken of in a natural and matter-of-fact way; but it must be treated with respect and even with reverence, because it is the means by which men and women are enabled to act on behalf of God in the creation of His children, which is why parents are said to procreate. The reason for not joking about sex is exactly the same as for not joking about the Holy Communion. It is not that the subject is nasty, but that it is sacred, and to joke about it is profanity. Moreover it is the point at which the spiritual and the physical come into closest interplay, and this no doubt is why moralists normally take it as the example of the moral struggle. Sexual sin is not the only sort of sin nor the worst kind of sin; the supreme sin and the fountain-head of all the others is pride, not lust. But if we let this function be used for our pleasure and amusement we are spoiling one of the most splendid things in the world.

We know the urgency of this matter. The Government has launched a campaign against venereal disease. We ought to take part in that campaign; and by all means let us do all we can to secure that those who are infected may by cured. But our share is more than that. We have to remind people that the one sure means of avoiding infection and of checking the spread of the disease is chastity. Almost exclusively this infection is contracted as a result of what is now called "promiscuous intercourse", but in the Bible and the Prayer Book is called "fornication". I think we have done harm by being so polite about these things. It is better to use the old language which disgusts people just because it disgusts them; for the thing is disgusting. All sensual indulgence outside matrimony is contrary to God's law and is sin. Let us be ready to say so. We need to build up an effective Christian public opinion on this subject. But remember that your opinion is not effective unless it is expressed.

I am perfectly sure that we shall not get the moral recovery we need except by a sense of obligation to God. We can do something on purely humanist lines: the rules of morality themselves are capable of a purely humanist defence; but there is no compelling power in that defence—it is no more than dialectical: the compelling power comes from the sense that the standards which we accept and which we seek to impress upon others are not ours but God's, and it is this which justifies us in upholding them and demanding for them universal acknowledgment and obedience.

So we meet here to-day to utter a call to all Christian

people, but especially the men of our Church, to shew in their own lives the fruits of their faith, and especially to resist. whatever company they may find themselves in, all tendency to join in dishonesty or impurity of word or action; and at the same time we utter our call to our fellow countrymen who do not join us in confessing allegiance to Christ, to seek in Him, and the revelation of God which He brings, the power which can restore to this country something that it once prided itself upon and has gone far to lose: for it used to be said that an Englishman's word is his bond; and we took it as a clear sign of the corruption of the Italian people when goods could not safely be left in public places such as railway trains —but what we despised in our neighbours is now to be observed among ourselves. There is a danger that we may win the war and be unfit to use the victory. For the sake of our whole cause and for the sake of the service which we hope to render to mankind, let us who own the name of Christ be zealous in our loyalty, and let us so shew its fruits to the world that they may seek to know the secret we enjoy.

X

The Crisis of Western Civilisation[1]

RECORDED ON JULY 12TH, 1943, FOR BROADCASTING
ON THE OVERSEAS SERVICE

IT is now universally recognised that this war is something
much greater than a conflict between two groups of nations
for a larger share of wealth and power. All can see that it
is a struggle between the adherents of two completely opposed theories of life. The United Nations are standing,
though with great variations of emphasis and of interpretation, for freedom, justice and supremacy of moral law; the
Axis Powers stand for the State as an object of supreme
allegiance and as a concentration of power unamenable to
any higher authority or law. This latter is no novelty among
men. It has been believed and practised by more persons and
over a longer period of time than the other; it is the creed and
practice of barbarism. The outlook to which the United Nations are, with variations, committed was generated in
Europe under the combined influence of Rome with its respect for law; of Greece with its ethico-political philosophy,
and especially the Stoic form of this, which spread through
the Mediterranean world the notion of a Law of Nations to

[1] This address is also published by Messrs. George Allen & Unwin, Ltd.,
in a series entitled *Crisis of Western Civilisation, and Other Broadcast
Talks.*

which all are subject; and of Palestine with its insistence that all Law derives its authority from God, who is Himself righteous, so that the laws of the State and the laws of the Universe can and should be in perfect harmony with one another. This association of man's personal and civic obligation with the ultimate power in the Universe is the special contribution of Israel, and was taken up into and reinforced by the Christian interpretation of divine righteousness as fulfilled in love, that love being expressed and thereby exercising an altogether new influence through the divine self-sacrifice of Calvary.

The fusion of these three elements, at once different and harmonious, led to the Christian tradition of Western Europe, and consequently also of the Western World. This rests on certain postulates which are indispensable but are often ignored. The first is the essential unity of the whole created order—or, if you like, of nature, including human nature. Man may be more than a part of nature, but he is that. At every turn he is dependent on his natural environment, and if he is to prosper in the long run it must be as a partner with nature in the production and utilisation of its resources, not as its lord exploiting nature for his own ends; that way leads to sterilisation and death. This partnership with nature did not have to be emphasised in earlier times because it was so evident and was everywhere taken for granted. It is the invention of machinery which has seemed to set a division between man and nature, making him appear to be at once its master and relatively independent of it. That is, of course, an illusory appearance; but it is one to which modern civilisation gives rise, and which it is now necessary, as it was not necessary in former times, expressly to expose. Man, in the Christian as in the scientific view, is part of nature, having his own place in the one great scheme, which is the plan and purpose of the Creator.

But, secondly, that place is a special one; for while on the side of his bodily life man belong to nature, he alone among created things has the capacity and the need to choose the objects for which his strength shall be expended. We all recognise this difference. As G. K. Chesterton used to say, "No one asks a puppy what kind of dog it means to be when it grows up". This is the essential difference. Other animals have that element in reason which is called intelligence at least in some degree; they think out means to the ends which their specific nature prompts them to pursue. They do not choose what ends they shall pursue; man does; and it is in this choice of ends that he becomes morally responsible and capable of fellowship with God. His chief end is "to glorify God and enjoy Him for ever".

This involves the third postulate—that man, who on one side is part of nature and is as such a creature of a few years, is capable of and destined for fellowship with the eternal God. Consequently his choice of ends—his choice between good and evil—not only has consequences for his neighbours or for the society of which he is a member, but has eternal significance for himself and even for God. He and his conduct have therefore an importance which is far more than biological or social or political. He has an infinite value because God loves him—not because of any quality of his own apart from his relationship to God, but because God loves him. And this is the basis of his claim to freedom—his claim to be himself, to live his own life and fulfil his own destiny. This also is the ground of the primacy of justice among social and civic virtues. If I am a creature with a life-span of sixty or seventy years, I cannot count for anything over against the nation or the State. But if I am a child of God, destined for eternal fellowship with Him, I have therein a dignity with which the State can make no comparable claim. It is here that man's dignity resides, in a region where all are equal. In the English Coronation service the King is seated as the token of earthly royalty is placed upon his head; but he is kneeling when just afterwards he receives the effectual tokens of divine grace in the same manner in which any labourer in any village church receives them. At the point where alone man has true dignity he is completely equal to all his fellow men; his infinite value is of such a kind as to shut out all superiority.

So this which is the source of man's claim to freedom and to justice is the source also of democracy. This may take many social and political forms; but the heart of it is always trust in the ordinary man—and the test of it is not whether the majority prevails but whether the minority is given freedom to express itself and to become the majority if it can.

What makes the historical picture rather confusing is the fact that the implications of the Christian scheme were still being worked out when men began to neglect its principles. In particular the political implications, though emphasised by theologians, were not followed out in practice with any completeness in the Middle Ages; and the theological scheme was too inelastic to allow for new experiences. So the great fabric began to crumble. One department of life after another claimed autonomy, politics, commerce, art, education. So the State came to be thought of as an end in itself—a doctrine long held in Germany and nakedly proclaimed by the Nazis: the idolatry of the State. So too the accumulation of wealth became for business men an end in itself—a doctrine widely held in Great Britain and America: the idolatry of money. And as the commercial men said "Business is business" and the patriot said "My country, right or wrong", so the artists said "Art for art's sake", with the result that the impulse of Art was mere self-expression without any enquiry whether there was a self worthy, or even fit, to be expressed. And now Education is recognising as never before that its job is to develop personality, but refuses to guide its activities by any general conception of what personality is.

In each department the assertion of autonomy has led to great development; but in life as a whole it has led to chaos. Our task in the coming period is to lay hold on all the cultural and economic wealth which the epoch of departmentalism has developed and integrate it once more in a coherent pattern of life with some intelligent principle.

The need for this is urgent. Not long ago it was hoped by many that the human values of the old tradition could be preserved without that entire view of the world and of life under the cover of which they were first appreciated and were in some measure established. But the voices of these non-religious humanists sound rather plaintive to-day; they echo in our ears as the utterance of a dream long ago dissolved. The harsh realities of experience are too much for them.

Meanwhile the problems due to mass-production press upon us. Is the life of nations to be a struggle for markets so as to keep people and machines employed? Are those who happen to control natural resources in iron, coal and oil to establish a tyranny over all their neighbours, with peace or war among themselves as the interest of each may suggest from time to time? Or are we going to make an attempt on a new scale to integrate human life? And if so, what is the principle of that integration? Later speakers in this series will work out the answer in more detail. But behind all their suggestions will be the conviction that our hope is in an advance to a more faithful Christian discipleship than has yet been seen on any large scale. At least the Christian religion offers a principle of integration. It is the plain duty of Christians to live by it themselves, to think out its meaning for our modern world, and to commend it to others as the one hope of deliverance from intolerable evils and the means of entering upon a glorious inheritance.

XI

The Armour of God

BROADCAST ON THE NATIONAL DAY OF PRAYER,
SEPTEMBER 3RD, 1942

Put on the whole armour of God.
Ephesians vi. 11

WE need that armour. For this war is not one more of the many national dog-fights of which history is full. It is a struggle between two different conceptions of life. In other words, it is a spiritual war in which, because it started with an act of aggression, earthly weapons have to be used. But earthly weapons cannot win the spiritual war. If our weapons are earthly only, then, even when the enemy is beaten, the real war will not be won. We need those earthly weapons; they are indispensable; but we need also and even more urgently the spiritual weapons, the armour of God.

When St. Paul used this challenging phrase, he had been speaking of the spiritual warfare which all Christians are called upon to wage. "Our wrestling is not against flesh and blood, but against the principalities, against the powers, against the world-rulers of this darkness, against the spiritual hosts of wickedness in the heavenly places." He felt himself surrounded with a whole atmosphere of evil which threatened to stifle the soul. He saw a world where evil has vast power. It was not human beings against whom he struggled but great vicious systems, before which, or in the grip of which, human efforts are futile. So he turns to the armour of God. He remembers some pictures, drawn by the old prophets, of God Himself waging war upon His enemies; and he calls on us to put on the armour of God—not only the armour which God will give us but the armour which God Himself wears; for He is our fellow soldier.

It cannot be necessary after three years of war against Nazi Germany to insist on the fact that this is a struggle between different conceptions of life. Yet even now, when the outrages committed in Poland, Czecho-Slovakia and Yugoslavia, and the ruthless oppression of Norway, Holland, Belgium, Greece and two-thirds of France have provoked the horrified indignation of all civilised men—even now we find people who suppose that the Germans who order these things and who carry out those orders are ordinary wicked men doing what they know is wrong. That is not so. They believe it is right for them to do these things. They are possessed by a conception of life according to which it is right for them to do these things.

Here we see a vivid illustration of that principle which our countrymen find it so difficult to accept—that a false belief is worse than any wrong action, because it leads to innumerable wrong actions. How often we hear the old silly saying that it does not matter what a man believes, and that this is a private affair between a man and his Maker. Are you going to say that of the Nazi belief?—of the belief that God is most perfectly revealed in His Germans, and that any means by which they can establish their supremacy over others are right because that supremacy is the purpose of God? Is that a private affair between each German citizen and his Maker? The Bible was perfectly right when it represented idolatry as the worst of sins. To worship a false god is the worst thing a man can do—far worse than deliberate atheism, worse even than careless neglect of the true God when we know something about Him.

But we shall not kill this idolatry by beating the armies of the enemy. It may spring up again among men, or in some other nation, or among ourselves. We have not been altogether free from it in some earlier periods of our history.

So the first part of the armour of God is the shield of faith —actual living trust in the true God, whose nature and character are what we see in Jesus Christ. Now—are we trusting Him? The King calls us to-day to prayer and dedication; and if we obey his call and there is reality in our prayers and our dedication, these will not be for one day only. Trust in God expresses itself in prayer. If a man hardly ever turns to God for His help, that man is not trusting God very much. Trust and prayer go together. The prayers need not be long. Our Lord warned us against supposing that we should be heard for our "much speaking". But, however brief, the prayers of a man who trusts God are regular and frequent. So the test of the reality of the prayers you offer to-day will be found in the question whether you also pray to-morrow, and the next day, and the day after that. Everyone can do it. We can all turn our minds to God as we get up, and as we go to bed, and at many times during the day. I suggest as a brief prayer for our country, which is also an act of dedication, the words "O God make us worthy of victory". Multitudes now are using the strokes of Big Ben as they sound through our loudspeakers at nine o'clock in the evening for a remembrance of God and of our dependence upon Him. Are you doing that? If not, try to begin to-morrow, and then keep it up.

Of course we have, as a people, been letting ourselves drift away from God. People do not know the Bible as their fathers, and still more their grandfathers, did. And if you know nothing about God, of course you cannot trust Him. So as well as the shield of faith we must take up "the sword of the Spirit which is the word of God". And we shall find it full of one demand upon us—to repent, that is to give up our own self-centred way of looking at life and learn to look at it in God's way instead. And we need this urgently. Not only have we let ourselves drift into forgetfulness of God, but with that we have let some of our moral standards slip badly. I have been told by Judges of the High Court that they are forced to think that there is less care for honesty, less shame at dishonesty, than there was. The Christian standards of conduct with regard to sex are very widely ignored. Until the call of the war came, there was among us less sense than in our best periods, that duty comes absolutely first and pleasure or comfort nowhere in comparison.

To win the war is not enough. We long to make, this time, a true peace and a better world. We long to see the nations dwelling side by side as members of one great family, enriching one another by their varieties of material resources, of tradition and of culture. We long to see all citizens within each nation united in the fellowship of real brotherhood. We have an experience of that brotherhood in the war in our unity of purpose and in the fellowship of suffering, a fellowship lately brought home to us when the Duke of Kent died on active service, uniting the Royal Family with the simplest and humblest in the common sacrifice. But this real brotherhood of man can only be actual and lasting for those who know God as the one Father of all men, in serving whom they serve each other because His love embraces all.

We hope to see our armies marching across Europe, setting free the nations as they advance. Let us be sure that they take with them, and that we have in abundance to send with them, the only promise of true peace—a living faith in God our Father and theirs. Let us be sure that our countrymen who follow in the occupations of trade and commerce go in the spirit of co-operation rather than of rivalry. But for all this journeying towards a friendlier and happier world we must have our "feet shod with the preparation of the Gospel of peace".

So then "put on the whole armour of God that ye may be able to withstand in the evil day, and having done all to stand". Clothed with the armour of God, we can call all men to dedicate themselves to His service as we dedicate ourselves this day.

XII

From the Old Year to the New

BROADCAST ON SUNDAY, DECEMBER 27TH, 1942

> Comfort us again now after the time that thou hast plagued
> us, and for the years wherein we have suffered adversity;
> shew thy servants thy work and their children thy glory.
> *Psalm* xc. 15–16

IT is the last Sunday evening of the Old Year, and with
Christmas still in our hearts and minds we look forward to
the New Year. The Old Year brought us searching tests—
a long series of reverses in the war, long periods of waiting
while nothing seemed to happen, then near its close the victory in Egypt, the triumphantly successful entry into North
Africa, the heroic self-immolation of the French fleet at Tou-
lon, the turning of Russia's stupendous stand at Stalingrad
into a victorious offensive. Every type of occurrence has
found a place in the Old Year's record, and each brought a
test of its own kind to the temper and spirit of our nation and
of our Allies.

Now when hope is brighter is the moment for vigilance,
for examination of the springs of our action in the deeper
regions of character; and when victory in a measure has
come to us and hope of final victory seems nearer, now is the
moment to set ourselves in the light of God's presence and
humble ourselves under His mighty hand. In days of reverse
and disappointment men tend to turn readily to repentance

and humiliation; but there is little merit in these moods at such a time and great likelihood of insincerity; for we may try to buy God's favour by our new recognition of Him and by the confession that we have not obeyed His law. It is rather in the day of apparent success and outward prosperity that the Christian will kneel before God and say, "Have mercy upon me, O God, after thy great goodness; according to the multitude of thy mercies do away mine offences". For the Christian knows that prosperity may breed forgetfulness of God, success may lead to pride and boasting, and victory brings with it responsibility for the use of it, for which our spiritual resource may be unequal.

So at this moment of passage from a year of so great vicissitudes, which yet closes with great hope and promise, to a year which must call for all we have of constancy in endurance, and perhaps also for the vision and wisdom to make a right use of success, let us take stock of ourselves and ask how far we, to whom a noble cause has been entrusted, are worthy to be its champions.

We have much, amazingly much, for which we ought to be thankful both in outward events, such as the deliverances at Dunkirk and in the Battle of Britain, and in the spirit of our whole people—their stedfastness, their good-fellowship, their unfailing humour. We have received from God great gifts; to pretend otherwise is not humility but perversity; to ignore the fact is not modesty but ingratitude. We thank God to-day for great deliverances and great gifts in the whole moral and spiritual constitution of our people.

But we must go on to ask if that is the whole story. The turn of the year is, as I said, a time for moral stock-taking in order that we may develop what is good and correct what is wrong. For the most part each must consider how matters stand with himself, for the remedy is to be found in the individual's correction of his own defects; no wholesale methods are possible in the sphere of character.

I begin with a saying made to me about two months ago by a prominent man with good opportunities for observation: "This war is being run on lure and bribery, not on service and sacrifice". Is that true or false? Or how far is it true? Of course there has been much sacrifice and an abundance of hard work. But how far is concern for dividends and wages uppermost in our attitude to all the activity which maintains our fighting Forces? Can our Russian allies teach us something here? I am not going to answer; that would do no good. The only answer that is of any use is the answer of each man's own conscience.

We have been and are being most wonderfully supplied with food. Do we let this conceal from our minds the appalling facts with regard to the hunger of some parts of Europe? Are we allowing true sympathy for those sufferers to spur us to yet more effort to hasten the victory which will set them free and give them food once more? Or are we in danger of complacency because our own comforts and amusements are so amazingly preserved? During the last war, it is said, Bishop Gore was once asked to say Grace before a meal at which the food supplied was very ample, and promptly said, "O Lord forgive us for feasting while others starve". Do we feel like that as much as Christians should?

Have we tried to picture what Hitler and Himmler are doing to the Jews of the nations they control? and do we let irritation at the distinctive ways of some Jews in our own country quench the flame of burning indignation that ought to kindle us to the most generous sympathy and efforts to help at whatever cost?

Do we maintain a strict code of honour with regard to rationed goods? or are we ready to gain advantages if we can for ourselves and for our friends beyond the limits set by a law which is framed in the best interest of all? I have heard a Judge of the High Court say that the standard of honesty among us has declined; are we trying to be rigidly honest in our own dealings?

Are we regulating our own lives with firm discipline? We have all heard of Regulation 33B; whatever we think of that Regulation, we know that the Minister of Health framed it because of the alarming increase of venereal diseases. Those diseases spread, with negligible exceptions, only through one means. If men and women avoided wrong indulgence, the danger would disappear. What is our own standard about this matter of sex—in our own conduct? in what we expect of our friends? in our conversation? Let each ask himself or herself those questions.

And as a root question bearing upon all the others, do we honour God? Certainly fewer people have been taking part in public worship than, say, thirty years ago. There are many reasons for this, not all of them discreditable. But does it mean that there is less regard paid to God, to His demand not only for goodness as we usually think of it but for holiness, to His love that finds no adequate expression except in Christ and His Cross, to the power to respond to that love and meet that demand for holiness which He gives to those who live by constant trust in Him? Is there less regard for these things? How much attention are you giving to them? How often do you turn your mind that way?

As the New Year draws near with its brighter hopes of evil forces vanquished and peace restored, will you try to be worthy of the opportunity which citizenship in this great nation and empire gives you? By yourself you cannot succeed. The greatest and most disastrous of errors is to suppose that we in our own wisdom can put the world to rights. If it were put right for us, our selfishness would put it wrong again in a fortnight. No; our hope must be in God; and our reliance must be on God. He is ready to use us; He is ready to make us fit for Him to use. For that very purpose Christ was born on the first Christmas Day. But as then He was weak and helpless, depending on His mother's love, so now He will not force His Kingdom on the world, for it is to be a reign of love calling out love. To establish it He died; but for us to become its citizens He waits, till our selfish hearts are broken by the patient pleading of His pain.

O God our Judge and Saviour, set before us the vision of thy purity and let us see our sins in the light of thy countenance; pierce our self-contentment with the shafts of thy burning love and let that love consume in us all that hinders us from perfect service of thy cause; for as thy Holiness is our judgment, so are thy wounds our salvation.

O satisfy us with thy mercy and that soon; so shall we rejoice and be glad all the days of our life. Comfort us again now, after the time that thou hast plagued us and for the years wherein we have suffered adversity. Shew thy servants thy work and their children thy glory.

XIII

Christmas: I

BROADCAST TO CANADA ON DECEMBER 20TH, 1942

WE are looking forward to Christmas—the most human of festivals which yet recalls the profoundest mystery of religion. It is the time when children look for presents in stockings which Santa Claus has filled, or sing their carols as the tree is lighted up. It is also the time when worshippers offer adoration to the Word made flesh. We miss its meaning and its value if we let either of these thoughts sink into the background.

There is little danger that we shall forget the human side of Christmas; and even if we did, so long as the deeper meaning of Christmas is understood, it will give rise to these more intimate festivities as it gave rise to them before. It is inevitable that the birthday feast of the Holy Child should be a feast for children, and that our thought of the Holy Family should both cause and hallow family reunions. Let us omit no part of all that makes Christmas the festival of home, which conditions enable us to observe. But let us be very sure that we keep in mind the deeper truth from which all our celebrations spring.

There is always some danger that the very beauty of the Christmas story may lead us to let our keeping of Christmas be an interlude of joyful fancy inserted between the claims and cares of this harsh world; that we should make it an excuse to withdraw from the harsh realities of the world into a dreamland of unreal beauty. Then it may no doubt bring joy while it lasts and some refreshment to weary spirits; but it will bring no inspiration or new strength; that can come only from what is as real as the duty to be done or the burden to be carried.

So we go back to the familiar story. So long as it deals with shepherds abiding in the field, or with the manger cradle, it is idyllic enough. But we must not isolate this. Mary and Joseph came to Bethlehem for the census which the Roman governor had ordered; and though the Empire of Rome stood for justice and order more than any which had preceded it, yet it was founded on conquest and its finance was systematised extortion. And by the grace of Rome, Herod was on the throne, a despot less amiable even than the average of persons called "the Great". That world was a hard and callous world. The Christian imagination has been fully justified in finding a symbolic meaning in the fact that for the Child Jesus and His mother "there was no room in the inn".

There is tragedy in the Christian Gospel; it is not the last note nor the prevailing one. The last and prevailing note is triumph. But the tragic note is there; the tragic element in life is fully accepted as a most terrible reality. Indeed this is what makes the triumph so complete. It is a victory won over evil at its worst; the everlasting light breaks out of the blackest darkness of historical gloom. And from the outset the sombre note is heard—Rachel mourning for her children and refusing to be comforted because they are not; the prediction to the mother of Jesus, "a sword shall pierce through thine own soul also". For all those parents who to-day are sad and shrink, perhaps, from the Christmas festivities because of the faces they will miss, there is in the Christmas story itself the touch of fellow-feeling, the companionship of true sympathy.

Above all the overwhelming splendour the Gospel of Christmas consists in precisely this—that the Lord of glory of His own will entered into our life of grief and suffering, and for love of men bore all and more than all that men may be called to bear. It is this fact which leads us to say that love came down at Christmas. If all that happened was that a baby was born who would grow up to be a wonderful teacher, then Christmas takes its place among the birthdays of great men; it is not then the festival of divine love. Of course this central Christian belief baffles intellect and holds imagination fascinated. It is either true or false; it is not to be thought of chiefly as beautiful, or inspiring, or comforting. The first question to be asked is—Is it true or false? for much of its beauty and all its power to comfort or inspire comes from its truth. And then how overwhelming the wonder is—

> That the Great Angell-blinding light should shrinke
> His blaze, to shine in a poore Shepherd's eye;
> That the unmeasur'd God so low should sinke,
> As Pris'ner in a few poore Rags to ly;
> That from his Mother's Brest he milke should drinke,
> Who feeds with Nectar Heav'ns faire family,
> 　That a vile Manger his low Bed should prove,
> 　Who in a Throne of stars Thunders above;
>
> That he whom the Sun serves, should faintly peepe
> Through clouds of Infant flesh! that he, the old
> Eternall Word should be a Child, and weepe;
> That he who made the fire, should feare the cold,
> That Heav'ns high Majesty his Court should keepe
> In a clay cottage, by each blast control'd;
> 　That Glories self should serve our Griefs and feares,
> 　And free Eternity submit to yeares.

It is this tremendous faith that can nerve us to the conquest of the evil in the world and carry us forward to the better order which all long to see. "This is the victory which overcometh the world, even our faith." If we turn our back upon the evil of the world and try to ignore it because it is so horrible, we cannot ever conquer it, and it, remaining unconquered, will continue to corrupt and corrode our lives. If we face it honestly, we are bound to be almost paralysed by horror and to recognise that we can at best do no more than erect against it very precarious defences. Our experience in these last years, as we have watched events in Germany and in the countries she has occupied and tortured, discloses such an abyss of evil in human nature as we never feared even in dreams to see.

But if God, the Almighty and Eternal God, has shared our experience in its depths of weakness and pain, and out of this has won a power that increasingly lays hold of men's hearts and wills, not overriding their freedom but using it as the way of approach to the citadel of their being, then there is hope. We do not have to conquer this evil world in any strength of ours; in spite of its brave showing, it is a beaten thing; and if we treat it so, in our own hearts or in the world outside, it will crack and crumple and dissolve.

We can do this only if our eyes are open to see power at the heart of weakness, the glory of God in the baby lying in the manger. "The Word was made flesh and dwelt among us." That is the divine fact. But it could become the focus and pivot of history only because there were some who, at least as they looked back, could say "We beheld His glory, glory as of an only begotten Son from a Father". St. Paul finds the touchstone in the Cross; it is to them that are perishing foolishness, but to them that are in the way of salvation the power and wisdom of God. But the principle which finds its clearest expression in the Cross is present throughout the Gospel story and in every moment when it is preached again. The divine fact is there—the Power that made the world dependent for life itself upon the care of those whom He had made; to worshippers of Force or slaves of Common Sense this is ridiculous. But the Power of Love is greater than the Power of Force, for it can break and re-make the hard hearts of men and women, and force cannot do either.

It is, then, no irony that in the midst of this clash of the mightiest armaments ever devised, from every quarter of the globe men are turning their thoughts to the stable of an inn at Bethlehem where a helpless Infant is lying. Multitudes who cannot on Christmas Day join in any service will join with the worshippers in the Churches, even, it may be, in the midst of battle, saying in their hearts, "Let us go even unto Bethlehem"; "O come, let us adore Him". For He who lies there in His helplessness, and because of His helplessness, is the King of Glory and of Peace. When we have thrown back the tyranny that threatens the whole world, it must be as subjects of that King, as worshippers of that Infant, that we set our hands to the tasks of peace and the fashioning of human fellowship. Our strength must be used in service of His weakness; our pride must be subject to the control of His humility; our selfish hearts must be penetrated and then filled by the energy of His love, if we are to be worthy of our task as defenders of human freedom or use our opportunity of fulfilling freedom in fellowship.

So we will sing our hymns and carols with more joy this year, not less; we will join in the children's festival with more hilarity, not less; but above all, there shall be in our hearts and minds more wonder at that love which excels all other love, more awestruck adoration of the central mystery alike of history and of faith—that He who is God of God "came down from heaven and was made man".

XIV

Christmas: II

CHRISTMAS has a hold on our affections which no other season of the year can claim. It may have won this partly by means of the happy gatherings which we remember from our childhood, and which we try year by year to reproduce in the changed conditions of later life. Members of a family scattered in many parts of the world exchange greetings; friendships are kept alive by the letters which pass at that season and, perhaps, at no other. All human ties are recalled and valued at Christmas; and the world would be infinitely the poorer if the keeping of it faded out.

All this wealth of wholesome human sentiment has its focus for Christians, and its origin for those who are not Christians, in the scene at Bethlehem where a mother put her Child to rest in the feeding-trough of an animal because the town was crowded and the rooms of the inn were full. It is that Child with His mother and foster-father who has brought to the world this yearly re-knitting of friendships and family reunions. His is the only birthday which is kept in every nation under heaven—and this birthday is so kept by at least a few people in every one. It is immensely worthwhile to recall the origin of our Christmas festivities. If we cut the connection between our own family gatherings and that little Family at Bethlehem, our gatherings will slowly lose their quality and then peter out.

How completely foolish anyone would have seemed who had said that first Christmas night that what was happening then would be remembered by an ever-widening circle of people till Christmas carols were sung clean round the world! It is so seldom that the most important things attract any attention when they happen. Suppose the Angels had gone to Augustus in his palace at Rome instead of to the shepherds on the hill-slopes of Judea. We do not know what he was doing that night; he may have been resting while some educated slave read to him a recent poem of Virgil's. But let us imagine him receiving a report from one of his distant Procurators—some Governor of an Imperial province—with stories of wild tribes beyond the frontier who threatened to attack and imperil the Roman peace. The Emperor has his chief counsellors and his military chiefs about him. They are anxious and perplexed; and we know they have reason for this, because some dozen years later a whole great army was to be lost on one of those frontiers, so that the old Emperor would fast on the anniversary of the disaster and would sometimes be heard to cry "Varus, Varus, give me back my legions".

It was all quite genuinely important—most important. But it was not so important as what happened that night at Bethlehem. Let us imagine those Angels coming to Augustus with his statesmen and his generals, and saying: "You are right to be anxious and to take every precaution; but what you are thinking about is not the most important thing that is happening now. After a few centuries only a handful of scholars will care about your frontiers problem. But with every century that passes a greater multitude will be singing with joy for this other thing." "What other thing?" they might say; and the Angel would answer, "All you could understand about it is that a poor woman in a very minor province has had a Baby".

That was what had happened; and now we all turn in worship to the Child who lies helpless in the stable. It is there—not in armies and policies—that the world finds a focus of its unity. The armies and the policies, like the guardians of Augustus' frontiers, have their own place; just now it is an indispensable place. The opportunity has to be secured and safeguarded for the growth of a fellowship of men throughout the world, grounded in this turning of all eyes and hearts to the Child at Bethlehem.

Augustus was hailed by his contemporaries as divine and it was widely believed that the peace and unity of the known world was due to him. He was, by comparison with other dictators, a merciful and gentle ruler. But his empire not only used force to maintain order; it had been won by force and rested on force. Other attempts of the kind had been made before and have been made since. They always fail; they always must fail; because they do not carry the hearts and wills of their subjects. The Child who was born at Bethlehem would be no warrior fighting his way to world-empire and divine honours; He would live by a love so perfect that though He died, despised and rejected of men—rather because He so died, He was recognised by His followers as God become man for love of men, and by that love winning an empire over men's hearts and wills—an empire therefore indestructible.

We are once again called to destroy an empire based on naked force; but the hope of the world will not be fulfilled when that is done; that hope will be fulfilled when the lesson of Christmas is fully learnt and we all submit our ambitions, our desires and our policies to the Love which came down at Christmas to live among men, the Child of Bethlehem.

XV

Good Friday, 1943

A B.B.C. "POSTSCRIPT"

ONCE again I am speaking to you from my own study; and I am speaking to you to-day because to-day is Good Friday, the day on which Jesus Christ was killed. Why is it called Good Friday? Why not, rather, Bad Friday? For surely it was a bad thing to kill the best man who ever lived. Certainly if that were all that could be said about it, Bad Friday would be a better name for it than Good Friday.

But that is not all that can be said about it. The most important part is left out. He who died on the Cross was not only a supremely good man; He was God—the Almighty and Eternal God—living a human life and dying a human death.

"That only makes it worse," someone may say; "if it was bad to kill the best man who ever lived it was still worse to kill a man who was also God." Yes: it was the worst thing that ever was done; and yet it was the best thing that ever happened. What the Chief Priests and Pontius Pilate did was the worst thing that ever was done; but what God did in Jesus Christ was the very best.

There was the perfect Love, which is the very nature of God, living among men as perfect love must and as nothing else can. And the selfishness of men reacted against it with increasing antagonism till at last men were crying out

106

"Crucify him! crucify him!" Yet the love never failed. There were no curses for His murderers nor bitter words for His torturers. No; His prayer was "Father, forgive them; they know not what they do". Against that perfect love the selfishness of men exerted all its strength. But the love remained unshaken, victorious, triumphant. It is because of that divine achievement that we call to-day Good Friday. It is the day when the Love of God shone forth in its fullest splendour. It is the day when the victory of love over selfishness and hate was won.

The fruits of that victory are increasingly gathered in as history goes forward. Our Lord had said, "I, if I be lifted up from the earth, will draw all men unto me"; and it is to the Cross on which He was lifted up that they are drawn. From all the world they come; from China and Japan; from Germany and Britain; from every country, however bitterly estranged from one another these may be, men turn to the Cross of Christ and are united as they worship there. So it is the well-spring of peace for all the world; for it is the magnet by which God draws our steely hearts away from their selfish ambitions into the fellowship of His own love. He who hangs upon the Cross is God; what we see there is what our selfishness means now to God. The Cross is the pledge of what God is to-night. We live, and work, and please ourselves in the presence of that God—of God who so loved and so loves the world, who so suffered and so suffers because His love is met by selfishness like ours.

To-day as always that love is calling to us. We need its secret. In every quarter of the earth men long to be delivered from the curse of war and to find in a world which has regained its peace a respite from the harshness and the bitterness of the world they have known till now. But so they often want the Kingdom of Heaven without its King, the Kingdom of God without God; and they cannot have it.

The Cross makes its appeal to all nations—Turn to God;—to all nations, and therefore to our own nation.

Things are not altogether well with us. We thank God for the splendid qualities our people have shewn—courage in danger, comradeship in service, perseverance in effort. But the decline in honesty has been very sharp and steep. Our standard of conduct in matters of sex is very lax. These things will bring terrible consequences if we will not change our outlook, or in the old phrase "repent". Think of some of the dangers of our slackness about sex—homes broken up, children without the care they need, venereal disease spreading at an alarming pace. Then recall the beautiful words in which just over a week ago Her Majesty the Queen spoke to the women of Britain about the noble contribution they are making and their supreme service in preserving the home and family life to which sailors, soldiers and airmen hope to return, and in creating the homes of the future. And men who are absent from their homes must remember that they have the same duty of faithfulness as their womenfolk at home. On every side the common welfare depends on the standard accepted and followed by each of us individually.

But every time we shall find that our selfishness is too strong for us if we try to fight it by ourselves. Turn to God—that must be our resolve; turn to God, whose love we see most fully in Christ upon the Cross.

We make plans for the future—for peace among the nations and for social security at home. That is right enough, and to neglect it would be wrong. But all our plans will come to shipwreck on the rock of human selfishness unless we turn to God, not once only and then turn away again, but in daily

ecollection of His righteousness and His love, in daily re-
iewal of our dependence upon Him. That is the way onward
ind forward to the only kind of new world order worth hop-
ng for. Turn to God, the Creator and Ruler of the world;
urn to God who so loved the world that He came to share our
iature even to the bitterness of death; turn to God who is
eady to direct and rule our hearts if we open them to Him by
3ible-reading, by prayer, by communion. Turn to God—that
s the chief need of England, and of every one of us. And for
hose who come there is no disappointment, if what they seek
s not some gift to satisfy a selfish wish, but just to be with
Iim and to serve Him, who loves us all with the love He
howed us on the Cross.

XVI

The Church Looks Forward: I

A SPEECH DELIVERED IN THE ALBERT HALL, LONDON
ON SEPTEMBER 26TH, 1942

ONE way of describing the purpose with which we are me
would be to say that we are here to affirm the right and th
duty of the Church to declare its judgment upon social fact
and social movements and to lay down principles whic
should govern the ordering of society. It has, of course, al
ways been recognised that the Church is called upon to la
down principles for the government of individual life. Wha
has lately been questioned—though by no means always in th
history of Christendom—is the right of the Church also t
lay down principles for the conduct of great corporations c
people—trade unions, employers' federations, national State
and the like—and to exert its influence not only upon the wa
in which men and women behave in society, but upon th
structure of society itself. But that division between the indi
vidual and the social groupings in which our lives are con
ducted, is quite untenable. Our lives are social through an
through. It is possible, no doubt, to lay excessive emphasi
upon the social as against the individual, as also upon th
individual as against the social aspects of life; but the two ar
intimately bound together, and whatever touches human lif
touches both.

The Church has this right, because in the revelation en

110

rusted to it, it has an understanding of man and his destiny
dependent upon that revelation, which illuminates every phase
of human conduct. But it has not only a right, it has a duty.
It has a duty to proclaim the principles that are involved in
the Gospel of Christ for the ordering of man's life, and that
duty is first and foremost to our Lord Himself. It is not first
and foremost a duty to society, as though society had a claim
to seek guidance from it. No doubt society does sometimes
turn to it for guidance, and when that happens—at least, very
often—we find that what is really wanted is that men should
be told how they may escape the consequences of their sins
without troubling about the sins themselves; and in all that
the Church has no interest whatever. But it has an obligation to Christ, the Lord of All Life, to proclaim His teaching
in all its fulness, and to show the blessings for human life
which follow from the acceptance of that teaching and from
adherence to it.

I suppose the objection that certainly does exist very widely
to this enterprise of the Christian Church mainly arises from
the risk that the Church may try to impose upon a society,
consisting of people of very various religious convictions and
none, a way of life or a system of organisation which is only
appropriate to those who are already perfect Christians. And
if we attempt simply to deduce from the ethics of the Gospel
what ought to be done in the political sphere, we shall very
likely fall into that blunder; but if we attend to the whole
range of Christian teaching we shall be safe from that, for it
is part of the Christian conception of man that unless he is
guided by, and is trusting to, the Grace of God, he is quite
incapable of conforming his life to the Divine Pattern. And
so our first duty is always to proclaim the fundamental Gospel
itself, and to call men to heed that, and then to draw out the

judgments that are implicit in it upon the order of society we know, and indicate the direction at least in which it seems that our forward move must be conducted.

We have then this duty—a duty to Our Lord—and we must approach our task always as in that spirit: not chiefly as bewildered citizens groping for a solution to a problem, but as the trustees of a revelation who go out into the world calling men to accept and follow it.

It would not be possible in a discourse of this kind, and especially in only the opening part of it, to set out the social principles that are implicit in the Gospel. It has been done many times over, and the upshot may be taken for granted in an audience of this kind. But when in the light of those principles we turn to the society we know, we find at any rate two points—and I have no doubt many more—at which we are bound to challenge that social order and to pronounce condemnation upon it. The first is the broken fellowship of our national life—what Disraeli called "the two nations". Of course it is true that at the moment, and under the stress of war, we are all united; we have a purpose now which binds us all together, and in the service of it we can lay our differences to rest. But we also know that that condition is not permanent, and indeed we are hoping for its early termination. The seeds of division are all there, and will spring up again and bear their bitter fruit unless we are ready for the new opportunity, and are prepared to set our feet on a new way. What is the source of these divisions? Our Lord told us with great clearness to seek first God's Kingdom and His justice, and then everything else would come right of itself —what we now speak of as economic distribution—what in the simpler, more direct language of the Gospel is spoken of as "what ye shall eat, what ye shall drink, the wherewithal ye shall be clothed". And so soon as we all desire that every man should have enough before each of us should himself have any superfluity, of course everyone would have enough. If we cared more for justice than for comfort and for luxury, economic distribution would be well on the way to solve itself. There would still be problems to be worked out; we should need the skill of the economists and of administrators; but they would find no insuperable difficulties.

Careful readers of the New Testament have often been surprised when they find St. Paul placing among the works of the flesh alongside the obvious carnal indulgences, envyings, strife, seditions; but by "the flesh" he means an outlook upon life which is mainly concerned with material goods. Here I must state once more, although I am getting tired of saying it, the old principle that is so fundamental, that material goods are limited in amount at any one time, so that it is true that the more one has, the less there is for other people; and if these are what we are aiming at, one man's success means other people's failure. It is not quite true with economic wealth, because it largely consists of credit, and credit is largely composed of moral factors. It is true of all purely material things: you must spread butter thin if you want it to go on a lot of bits of bread. But it is not true of the good things of the spirit, indeed of all those good things which we enjoy by our distinctively human faculties. It is not true of knowledge—that imparts itself: it is not true of the appreciation of beauty—that is infectious: it is not true of courage, which is more infectious still: it is not true of love and joy and peace—wherever these find a home they spread all round about it. And so when men put first the good things of the spirit they are always brought into fellowship, because here one man's success is everyone else's success; but when they put first material goods they will always be brought to divisions, strife and enmity, and the broken fellowship of our life rests in the last resort upon the materialism of our everyday outlook. We must bring that to an end. From it flow all the great evils that afflict us in our social life; from it flow, in the last resort, our unemployment, that canker of modern society, and that absence of real leisure for those who are in employment under the economic system. One of our first aims must be to supply adequate real leisure to all sections of the community: but remember that the only difference between leisure and unemployment is whether you have some money to spend.

And the other point to which I want to draw attention today is a different expression of the same principle. The predominant motive governing the whole process and the direction of industry is what is for short called "the profit motive". Now it is quite true—at least I think so—that there is no harm in the profit motive as such. It is perfectly reasonable that a man should want to improve his own position—still more reasonable that he should want to give to his children a better chance than he had himself. It has its own right place, but that is not the first place. And it is the predominance of the profit motive—the fact that it comes first in the determination of so much of our economic and industrial activity that is a great evil: and the evil does not chiefly consist, to my mind, in the fact that it is an expression of self-interest and is therefore something lower than the highest, though not all self-interest is wrong (see Butler's admirable sermon on self-love). But when the whole policy of the economic world is governed chiefly by this motive, it results in a dislocation which cannot be corrected until another motive is supplied in the first place.

You consider such a problem, for example, as the location of industry. Where shall a given factory be built? And if the only consideration in mind is where it will be most profitable to build and work it, you will not have worked out any proper relationship between urban and rural life, and between industry and agriculture. And the working out of that balance is one of the great problems which should be engaging our attention in the coming time. But how can it be done if the decision is left to a body of people whose only bond of union among themselves—whose only basis of association—is the efficiency of the concern with which they are entrusted, which must, according to current habits, be judged by the profits that they make? And so the profit motive, whether it takes the form of concern about wages or about dividends—and it is just as much the profit motive when it is wages as when it is dividends—should never get into the first place. And yet you cannot expect to keep it out of that first place as long as you organise industry as it is organised to-day. However high-minded and public-spirited the Directors of a privately owned concern may be, they will, five times out of six, be bound to put first the purely economic interests of what they are working rather than the public interest; and, if they do put the public interest first, how are we to know that they are qualified to estimate it properly? They are not chosen for the purpose. They will quite rightly say it is not their function. If we want the public interest put first, we must so organise our life that those who are chosen for their concern with and qualification to judge the public interest, are in positions of control. And if we are to do this, if we are really to assert effectively the supremacy of the public interest over private, then there are two points where I think we need to take definite decisions, and they concern land and money.

There are four requisites for life which are given by the bounty of God—air, light, land and water. These exist before man's labour is expended upon them, and upon air and light man can do nothing except spoil them. I suppose if it were possible to have established property rights in air, somebody would have done it before now, and then he would demand of us that we should pay him if we wanted to breathe what he called *his* air. Well, it couldn't be done, so it hasn't been done. But it could be done with land, and it has been done with land; and, as it seems to me, we have been far too tender towards the claims that have been made by the owners of land and of water as compared with the interests of the public, who need that land and water for the ordinary purposes of human life. I am not myself at all persuaded that the solution of this problem is to be found in the nationalisation of land; but I am persuaded that we need to find ways of asserting the rights of the public over the interests of the private owners; and we come back here to the great Christian principle, that the right which attaches to ownership is a right of administration, but should never be a right to exclusive use. That is a principle deep and constant in the old Christian tradition about property, but we have so largely forgotten that property is in its own nature and of necessity a social institution and a social fact, that we have ignored the rights of society over against the rights of those to whom it entrusts ownership, and we must restore that balance. Incidentally, may I say that I think we should greatly welcome the Uthwatt Report just published? It seems to me to aim most hopefully at a combination of the advantages of public control and private initiative, but we shall have to watch and take care that its principles are not whittled away in concessions to vested interests. I am going on the assumption all through that it is not reasonable to expect that men are going to act always from the motive of service, and that what we have to do, if we can, is to secure that private interest becomes subservient to the public good. There was a period when people took it for granted that the two things coincide; they do not. And if they do not coincide, it is the public good that must prevail.

When we turn to money, we come to something in which our methods have changed greatly since a hundred, or even fifty, years ago. When there was a multitude of independent banks, it may, for aught I know, have been the most appropriate method of issuing credit that they should be mainly responsible for it; but with the amalgamation of the banks, we have now reached a situation in which what is a universal necessity—namely money, or the credit which does duty for money—is, in spite of keen competition in certain fields, on the way to become a monopoly. Now it is surely a primary political principle that, when something which is universally necessary becomes a monopoly, that monopoly should be taken under public control; and in my judgment at least—I don't claim that it is worth much, but I want to offer it you—in my judgment at least it should be now regarded as improper for any private person or corporation to issue new credit, as it was in the Middle Ages for any private person or corporation to mint actual money, for the two are equivalent. Of course, this is not in the least to censure our banks or bankers, who have worked the system entrusted to them with singular integrity, ability and public spirit; but they are working something which is now out of date and is become anomalous, and there has happened—what nearly always happens when you maintain an anomaly—that what should be your servant is become your master; and finance, which should be the servant of production, is become its director, while the consumer whose needs should be the sole end of production, is regarde merely as a necessary condition of producing profitably.

That leads me to my last point. Whatever may be though of the particular illustrations I have given, here we come t a fundamental principle. The root trouble with society is sir that strange perversion and fatality of human nature whic leads it to turn its blessings into curses, and we need befor all things else to call men back to dependence in a living sens upon the Grace of God. Let us never suppose that any exter nal readjustment of the structure of life can produce fellow ship or goodwill. No doubt there are some forms of huma society which suggest fellowship, and some which sugges rivalry; but whatever the outward form, the sin of men ma take hold of it and possess it, and that acquisitiveness i human nature, which at present expresses itself through ur limited search for material wealth, may just as easily expres itself in a collectivised society through the grasping an manipulating of the levers of power. And on the whole tha would be more disastrous for the other citizens than wha we have at present. At all times it is the primary duty of th Church to remind men that if they neglect God they cann make a success of human life. Only by following His way can it be done; only in His power can His ways be followe And, if this is to be so, if we are to bring social as well a individual life under the power of the redeeming love of Go then we must link up our worship with our social aspiration And so let us remind ourselves once more that in the Eucha rist, where we offer what is the fruit of man's labour expende upon God's gifts, bread and wine, in order that we may re ceive them back charged with His power and share them i perfect fellowship, we have always the perfect picture of th

Christian society. But we have been neglecting that aspect of our highest act of worship, and we must recover our sense of its meaning for the social life of man, as well as for the individuals who there receive the power by which they may follow the Lord in the way of love, even though it be the way of sacrifice. When worship is once more the consecration of all life, and when life itself, industry and commerce no less than family and friendship, is the expression of worship, then we shall see a Church fully alive and the fulfilment of our social dreams.

But there is a danger here—the danger that we may try to use God as a means to our end—and that is poison. We must set about this because we believe He calls us, in service of His purpose and in preparation for the coming of His Kingdom. And so the question in the last resort is one that comes home to every individual here or elsewhere. To each of us and each of those whom we can influence, the challenge comes: will *you* hear and heed the call of Christ? Will *you* day by day submit your thoughts and desires, your hopes and plans for yourself and for the world, to the directing influence of His Holy Spirit? In short, will *you* be His disciple in all parts of your life? And I trust our answer is one that can be expressed in the words of the old Mission Hymn —"Wave the answer back to Heaven, By thy grace—we will".

XVII

The Church Looks Forward: II

A SPEECH DELIVERED IN BIRMINGHAM
ON NOVEMBER 14TH, 1942

MY Lord Bishop, my Lord Mayor, your Excellency and my Friends,—My first duty must be to express the gratitude which I know that all of us who have come to speak at this meeting are feeling, to the citizens of Birmingham and the people of the neighbourhood for the wonderful welcome that they have given to us, and the degree of interest that has been shown throughout this part of the country in this meeting— the second of the series which began at the end of September in the Albert Hall.

And I also wish to say how immense is the encouragement that is given to the Archbishop of York and myself by the presence with us here to-day of the American Ambassador. I think all of us feel that the future of the world largely depends upon the close understanding and co-operation between the people of the United States and ourselves. But those of us who are gathered in a meeting like this are equally convinced that while the future must depend upon that, the welfare of the future depends upon this co-operation being directed along Christian channels; and that the Ambassador should be willing to come and join with us in advocating that cause is a source of the most profound encouragement, and an occasion for the deepest gratitude.

120

Well now, this meeting, as you know, is a follow-up in one sense, in what, as has been said, is the second city of this Province—and in magnitude at least, for I have loyalties elsewhere, in magnitude the second in the Kingdom—of a meeting that was held not long ago in the Albert Hall, and which attracted some public interest. Our concern is to proclaim to all whom we can reach the duty of the Church, to declare the Christian principles that bear upon social life. It has always been recognised, of course, that the Christian religion has its message for the life of the individual within the framework of society. We are concerned to insist that it also has its message for the ordering of society itself, and that the social structure, as well as the lives of individuals living within that structure, is subject to criticism in the light of Christian principles.

And so far I think that there is no opposition as a rule to that, so long as it is stated in general terms, until you begin to touch the sphere of economics; and then there is liable to be a loud cry of "Hands off". Now there is, of course, a reason for that. The reason is that there really is a science of economics, and that the business of the science is to study the causal laws which are operative in the economic sphere. And no degree of personal piety and no amount of theological learning will enable a man in the smallest degree to pronounce a competent judgment upon the probable actual effects of any economic action. That is all perfectly true, and when any ecclesiastic does enter that field, he ought, I think, to try to make it quite clear that he is expressing his personal conviction, and that he is not the spokesman at that moment of the Christian Church so that he can call upon others who claim the Christian name to agree with him.

One of the difficulties of this matter is that in the sum-mary necessary for press reports, these explanatory remarks made by a speaker are nearly always left out, and I have no doubt they will be to-day. You cannot help it; I do not blame either reporters or editors, or even that "monster" of a man I have never met called the sub-editor. They are often in great difficulties in reporting at all adequately in the space they can give, and they have to cut out what seems the least essential part. And so we have to put up with the fact that we are sometimes told we have proclaimed gravely controversial things as if they were part of the Gospel. Never mind, it cannot be helped.

Because what is perfectly plain is that you cannot get very much attention for or discussion of fundamental principles until you can also show people how you think that they would work out; and it is only by indicating the specific lines of action that you can claim attention to principles themselves. All the same, it is the principle, and only the principle, which the Church as such has any right to proclaim. The rest is merely illustrative matter, of which I shall be giving you a little later on; but it is only illustrative matter.

Well now, the main business of the Church in that whole realm must be to insist upon the distinction between means and ends, and it is largely through confusing means and ends that we have got into a large part of our troubles. Of course the distinction is not clean-cut or absolute; because there is only one ultimate end of man, and it is, as the Shorter Catechism puts it, "to glorify God and enjoy Him for ever". That is the chief end of man; and in comparison with that everything else whatever is relative. Everything else whatever has got in the last resort to be judged by the question whether it does help men towards the attaining of that one chief end. None the less, there are real ends in life, and they are all in that realm which belongs to us in virtue of our spiritual and intellectual capacities, and not of our animal capacities. They all belong to the realm, for example, either of knowledge, or appreciation of beauty, or friendship, or family affection or loyalties, and courage, and love and joy and peace. They are all, in fact, in the wider sense of the term part of the fruit of the spirit; and those, and those only, are real ends. The whole economic sphere is concerned with means to those ends; and it must be judged, not primarily by its efficiency within itself, by its effectiveness in promoting maximum output and the like; but primarily in the light of the question whether it is fostering the attainment of the real ends by the greatest number of people. We may take as our slogan, if you like: "Fulness of Personality in the widest possible Fellowship".

Of course efficiency is of very great importance. If an economic system is inefficient, if changes are introduced into it which impair its efficiency, the result will be poverty, want, and consequent unhappiness and restriction of the fulness of human life. The concern of the business man with efficiency in his business is a perfectly right concern; and no amount of sheer idealism will compensate for mismanagement. That is entirely true, and in its own place immensely important; but in its own place. It is the second place, and not the first. The first place is the kind of human life which is being rendered possible, or it may be which is being made necessary, by the type of economic system in which a man lives. And we shall therefore, in any criticism of the economic system itself, not only start firstly by asking whether it is capable of producing a greater output than any other that can be devised, but always first by asking whether it is promoting the best type of human life and of human relationship, both within the economic process itself and outside it; and recognising efficiency as having its importance, because it is necessary to this true human welfare.

We are living in days when the serious implications and possibilities of life are constantly before our eyes, and we may find it almost hard to recall what were quite familiar sounds and sighs in the days of peace. Visitors to our shores in those days used sometimes to twit us with issuing, for example, or those posters that might appear in connection with evening papers—"England's Downfall", or something of that sort; and what it would mean was not either that we have betrayed some great cause or that we had been defeated in battle— because there could not have been one—but that something had gone wrong with the Test Match in Australia. Now it may be true that we have exaggerated the importance of sport; but there is a healthy instinct behind that, because a game is an end in itself, at any rate if you really play it as a game. There are some people who turn games into a business, when the poison has got really deep into their system. But the object of a game is the game: there is nothing beyond it. When you begin looking for something beyond it, then you are ruining it. The reason why I gave up golf was that I began to wonder why I should care whether the ball went into the hole or not. It generally didn't. Well, once you begin to question, the game is ruined. You have got to take it mystically, or not at all; for it is an end in itself.

Politics are never an end in themselves. The whole arena of politics belongs to a class of activities which is less important than the class to which games belong. I do not say that politics are less important than games, because they are means to more important ends, while games are a less important end. And so politics are of more importance; but hey belong to that particular class which exist for something beyond themselves. That is supremely true of the economic part of political life; it is all concerned with the means by which men are to pursue virtue, religion and happiness. If we begin to think that the pursuit of economic wealth is a reasonable aim for a human being to set before himself as an end, everything will go wrong. You are treating as an end what is in its own nature a means, and all perspective will be falsified.

It is true that under the pressure in which we are living we have very largely done this thing. We have treated the production and acquisition of economic wealth as if it were the only end for man, and it is not. So everything has got into wrong perspective and wrong setting; and the first thing we have to do is to recall men to the appreciation of the real and true goods, which are ends in themselves and which the whole economic process exists to serve. And if we are thorough and in earnest about it, there is going to be a very revolutionary change of outlook. It means, for example, that while the economist has his special and indispensable place in telling us what are the probable effects of any proposed activities, that does not of itself give us any direction about what we should do. We still have to choose between the various goals of activity, and ask the economist how we may then best pursue them. But if we leave him to himself, he will inevitably keep maximum output first as the one true end, and it is not.

Now when we come to look at our present economic set-up in the light of such Christian principles, we find some undoubted defects in it, to put it mildly; and supremely we find that division which Disraeli spoke of as "the two nations"— the breach in our fellowship between the "haves" and the "have nots". Now what is it that some people have and others have not in our day? Not, I think, primarily material possessions, though that does come into it; not primarily the necessary basis of physical life, though we have not yet got that really secure in any universal way; but primarily security and power. These are two things of vital importance to men's happiness and welfare in life which are most unevenly distributed.

There does seem to be a general agreement that, as we work for the future, we must be doing our utmost to establish a reasonable measure of security for all persons in our economic order. You can never make it absolute; there is no absolute security in life for any of us. Any individual in this meeting may have a chimney-pot fall off on to his or her head as he or she walks home, and suddenly be sent to Kingdom-come. There is in life no such thing as absolute security. If it did become absolute it would be a very bad thing for us. But there are large proportions of our fellow citizens for whom the bottom is liable to fall out of life through no action of their own, but simply through the way in which our economic system is worked or works, and it is a shocking evil and we must fight against it.

The great mark of something being wrong is to be found in the cycle of unemployment which has been a feature of our economic life now for the last hundred years or more, and of which you have to take notice. For the intervals between the peaks of unemployment tend to become shorter, and the intensity of the evil when it comes tends to increase. That is the broad and terrible lesson of the last period. Let us take it to heart and say, "There is something wrong there that has got to be altered". Many would probably have wished that we had set about altering it before, and no doubt many more have now come to see that we must ensure that at all times the public interest prevails over any private or sectional interest when they clash. In principle there is not a direct conflict between them, because it is to the public interest that private interest should normally be secured. Of course any system which enables autocrats acting nominally for the public to override the private interests of any and every section at any and every time, would in fact be very contrary to the real public interest. But there are times when public and private interests clash, and we can see them, for example, in such a matter as land speculation, when there is likely to be an extension of some great city, or when there is need for rebuilding a destroyed area.

We have taken some steps to check such speculation. I doubt if the steps we have taken so far are in the smallest degree adequate. I do beg that all of us may become acquainted with the principles of the Uthwatt Report, and so pull up public opinion that it will require that, to the extent there recommended by a thoroughly responsible Commission, public interest is secured against all private depredations on it.

I think we have got especially to secure this supremacy of the public interest in the matter of land and water, and in the matter of credit. I have talked about credit before; but people do not always like it talked about. I do not ask you to believe anything I say about it; but I do ask you to think about it. And I do ask you further to consider whether we do not need specially to secure the public control both of the volume of credit and the direction in which it is issued from time to time. Of course in war-time we have got it. The point is, are we going to maintain, when the war is over, the authority by which the public hold that control now? And then in war-time there is another thing which seems to me absurd, and again I ask you to consider it. I do not state it as a dogma; but to me it seems ridiculous, when the nation needs credit for the carrying-out of its own purposes, that it should borrow that credit from a section of itself and pay interest on it. The source out of which repayment has to come is of course the whole national production. That is the real security, and I cannot see why anything more should be paid for it than the actual administrative cost, which a very high authority has told me is perhaps one-eighth of one per cent.

I do beg that there may be a body of influence guided by Christian principles that is exercised about these things, and that whatever conclusions we then reach as regards a particular policy to be adopted, we should be united in pressing forward along lines which are conducive to the real public welfare. I suggested just now one formula, but I want to suggest another. It is only a paraphase of the former—"Supremacy in all respects of the Human Person". And if we are going to make that our standard, then first we must secure that that human person is born in a house fit to be a real home; secondly, we must secure that that human person has the nutrition necessary for the full development of his or her physical capacity; and thirdly, we must secure that that human person until the age of maturity—that is to say, at any rate until eighteen—is primarily the subject of education and never primarily a factor in industry.

These three things first, and then I should wish to add to it that that human person should have his personality recognised by gaining a voice through his representatives in the control or direction of the concern in which he is occupied. But there is an outline of the first three things—housing, nutrition and education—which must be tackled for the fulness of development of every human person. Let them be our goal. You cannot get all that in the first year after the war. What matters is that you should know of the direction in which you mean to go, and then direct each step forward as soon as it is possible to take it. But you must know your direction first, and I suggest we should claim these first three things as instrumental to a realisation of and as indispensable to a full Christian civilisation.

One other word. We are told very often that the Church itself needs reform as much as anything else, and I quite agree that there is much calling for reform; and until we effect reforms in the structure of the Church the outside world will not listen to us as fully as it might. I am not going to say anything more about that, because the Archbishop of York is going to say a good deal upon that subject. Heaven knows what it is going to be, but I shall be out of the room before he says it, although I tell you in advance it is all true, whatever it is.

But Sir Stafford Cripps challenged us at the Albert Hall with this question: "Are you ready for Disestablishment and Disendowment?" And there are people within the Church who think that steps ought to be taken as a sign of our sincerity to make a direct move towards Disestablishment.

I am glad some people applaud that, because I want the support of such a stimulus; but I do not agree with them. If you are going into Disestablishment, it is an immensely intricate process; and a good many of us are going to be tied up, for five or ten years to come, merely to adjusting the machinery of the Church, and not getting on with our real job. But I say this very strongly, that I cannot see that the question of Establishment is any direct concern of the Church as such at all. It is the concern of the State; and it is a concern for us as Christian citizens influencing the State; and I believe there are values connected with Establishment for the life of the nation and State which would be lost by Disestablishment, and which would be hard to replace. But it is no concern of the Church. We have a divine commission; we exist as a divine creation. If the earthly State likes to associate itself with us, let it. If it would rather separate itself off, let it. But our business is to be true to the commission we have received: to proclaim unchanged the unchanging Gospel of God, and in every generation to try to show to people the implications of the unchanging Gospel to their changing circumstances. That is the Church's task for every succeeding generation. Let us see to it that we do thoroughly and fully, and at whatever cost, show loyalty to our commission.

XVIII

The Church Looks Forward: III

AT previous meetings in this series I have said that the purpose of them is to declare the Church's duty to state the principles which for Christians should govern political and social action. I find from the comments which reach me that there is need to put this matter also from another point of view, and therefore I have asked leave to speak this evening on the religious quality of the great political issues. For what is really required is an extension of the meaning which we give to the word "religion". Of course the inner heart of it must always be the relationship between the soul and God. Without that, even though right principles are proclaimed, there will be no driving power to effect their execution. But religion must not be confined to this inner core, because the relationship of the soul to God that is achieved through Christ is something which of its own nature is bound to permeate the whole of life and give direction to it. On one of the occasions when it was said afterwards that I had spent the whole of my speech on politics and not on religion, I had in fact been discussing what are the real ends in life and what activities have importance and value only as means to those ends. What I wish now to urge upon you is that that is a fundamentally religious consideration, because if we have any religion at all, it must supply us with a hierarchy of ends and means to them, giving the primacy to some and giving to others an entirely subordinate place.

The chief end of man is to glorify God and enjoy Him for ever, and all discussion of objects to which it may be worth while to devote time and strength must be conducted in the light of that fundamental conviction.

Then subordinate to that are the various types of social objectives which must always be considered primarily from the point of view of the fatherhood of God and the brotherhood of man. All that promotes the development of truly personal qualities in human life and binds people together in real community has its place within the divine purpose. Everything which tends either to stunt the development of personality or to set people at variance with one another, so breaking up the community of the family of God, is contrary to the divine purpose. It must be with thoughts like these that we approach the consideration of the reconstruction of Europe or the establishment of social security at home; and if we do so approach them, then our discussion, for example, of the principles of the Beveridge Report, becomes a specifically religious discussion.

This war should have made clear to us the religious quality of great political issues, because the main question at stake in this war is a religious or theological question. In fighting to preserve the traditional qualities of European civilisation and to keep open the way for developing these to their true fulfilment, we are really fighting for the status of every man and woman as something independent of membership in any earthly State, an independence which is only intelligible and, as I am convinced, can in practice only be maintained, on the basis of faith in God and an understanding of men and women as children of God destined for eternal fellowship with Him.

It is at once apparent that the whole question of the relation of the State to its subjects is profoundly modified by the giving of a positive or negative answer to the questions, Does God exist? Are men His children? No doubt it is true that there are very many people who actually value freedom without associating it in any way with faith in God; but their value for it is merely a personal liking; they have no real answer to the case stated by the philosophers of totalitarianism except that they prefer something else, and in the immense pressures of the modern world that preference will be a feeble bulwark for our threatened liberties. Let us remember that the threat of totalitarianism, with its reduction of the human being to a mere slave of the State, is not confined to those countries which have deliberately adopted a totalitarian creed. It results from the enormous concentrations of power which are the product of our new control over the forces of nature. Mass production of material goods and of popular entertainments, to some extent even of education itself, has an inherent tendency to depress the value of individuality and so to make the unity of the herd the only kind of practicable unity, in place of that fellowship which is the free union maintained by free citizens because of the value and richness of the life that they find in it.

Now if we are to order life according to these principles, in face of the great pressures that are playing upon us, we must in these days deliberately plan it, at least to some extent. It is quite true that every kind of planning involves the diminution of some liberties; but the chief enemy of freedom to-day is not an intelligent plan but the irresistible pressure of blind forces. We must gain control of those forces, and that involves planning. We need, for example, deliberately to plan the balance of industrial and agricultural life; otherwise when the war is over our agriculture will again be overwhelmed by external competition and we shall more and more find our population living almost exclusively in towns. This is bad for physical health; but it is still worse for moral health. We need a genuine balance of urban and rural, industrial and agricultural, and we can only obtain it by planning.

But then of course everything depends upon what we are planning for. Are we planning only for efficiency and maximum economic output, or are we planning for fulness of personal life in community? Is our primary aim to be material comfort, or responsible citizenship? Of course there is need for efficiency, and of course there is need for effective output; without these things we cannot have fulness of personal life and richness of community experience. But if we let the economic aim become predominant, we shall find that it disintegrates our society, that it treats every individual primarily as so much labour power to be used where he most conduces to efficiency of output, irrespective of all his social ties and traditional roots. The economic approach to life atomises society. The whole economic order is of vital importance, but it is important as a means to something beyond itself, and if its activities become the end of life or its organisation, the result is to sacrifice the ends to the means. And if we plan only for prosperity and comfort we may create a society which is comfortable, contented and spiritually dead. We must plan for freedom, for the exercise of responsible citizenship in real community.

Now if such planning is to work, we must have control of those factors which are indispensable to welfare in the modern world. The primary requisites of life are air, light, land and water. Air and light are still free. Over land and water we must establish a social control, whether or not this carries with it national ownership. (Personally, I believe that it need not and hope that it will not; but the control is essential.) Similarly, in the modern world we must have effective control of the issue of credit. The Government has in fact so largely entered this field that what is required is rather the acknowledgment of a principle already active than any revolutionary change.

But beyond all this we need supremely the control of human purpose. All this planning that we now see to be necessary can bring about genuine and free fellowship only if there is at work in the hearts of the people the spirit of genuine goodwill—and here is our fundamental need. How are we to find this spirit of goodwill, the spirit which genuinely prefers fellowship to domination and justice to gain? We know quite well that it is not natural to man in the sense that he possesses it from birth and will always display it unless circumstances are unfavorable. On the contrary, though there is in human nature an abundance of generosity and kindliness, there is at the very heart of this a self-concern which at any serious crisis becomes predominant. In those countries which have sacrificed everything to national unity there has been full recognition of the psychological principle that no group becomes effective unless it is gathered about a leader. Hitler's *Führer-Prinzip* is perfectly sound psychologically; and if we are to build up a community characterised by goodwill, it must be a community which has found as its leader someone who is Himself the incarnation of Goodwill. Here is part— perhaps the chief part—of the contribution which we as Christians ought to make to the new order—to make ourselves manifest in the world as a true community gathered about our Leader, who is the Lord of Life. Only let us recognise that whereas Hitler and other mob leaders appeal to people on their better and worse sides both at once, this Leader will appeal to us on the better side only, and we cannot follow Him wholeheartedly so long as our hearts are still partly selfish and partly mean; and therefore for the sake of the social redemption quite as fully as for individual redemption, we have still to preach the need of conversion and bring home the Gospel in all its power to the souls of individual men and women, not only that they may be saved when this world's history is finished, but in the fashioning of this world's history may be a living community gathered about and following through sacrifice and through triumph the Leader who is Himself Incarnate Love.

XIX

The Church Looks Forward: IV

A SPEECH DELIVERED IN EDINBURGH
ON JUNE 4TH, 1943

IT is a good while ago now that an observer of social developments summed up the situation in the saying "Things are in the saddle and they ride men". That is a way of expressing what is sometimes spoken of as the mechanisation of life and it vividly indicates the perverseness in our recent developments in many respects.

No one, I think, would be found to deny that we have to a quite large extent so concentrated upon the means to fulness of human life that we have developed them in ways making that development impossible. The whole situation is topsyturvy and contradictory. That is why we constantly have to go back to first principles and link these up with detailed practical schemes in a way which seems to many people to involve a confusion of things wholly different from one another. And yet there is no chance of sorting out the factors of our national and international life unless we are attending to the principles and the details at the same time.

As we are Christians, we go back to consider the purpose of God, and here there can be no doubt, for the purpose of God is quite plainly something that can be described in the formula "The development of persons in community". It is something with two sides to it, and the purpose will be frustrated if either of these receives exclusive attention—and of course behind this purpose is God Himself, and the purpose can only be fulfilled so far as it is recognised to be His.

This was the first break-away, so to speak, which put the modern development on wrong lines. The Renaissance seemed to the people who experienced it to be a wonderful liberation of human energies—as indeed it was—but it took the form, for quite clear historical reasons, of a dethronement of theology and consequent assertion of the supremacy of man. This pervaded human thought increasingly through the eighteenth century, and the men whose ideas and aspirations lay behind the French Revolution undoubtedly believed that man was able to take his destiny into his own hands and make of it something that would satisfy him. Men began to treat God and the relation of individuals to Him as a private matter having no public interest. The French political revolution was immediately followed by the English industrial revolution, which left the political structure comparatively untouched but affected the ordering of society far more intimately. And here once more there was a great sense of an expansion of human power. It depended upon the initiative and energy of individuals, and the aim of reformers was as a rule to throw off restraints in every direction. Individualism was triumphant and there was a widespread belief in the moral, social and political value of unfettered competition. This was reinforced by the quite unwarrantable interpretation of Darwinism as giving the clue to moral progress: for the survival of the fittest was taken to mean the survival of the best.

This headlong individualism which laid all the emphasis upon the development of persons tended towards complete economic anarchy, and secured in fact freedom of action and development for a few persons at the price of condemning the majority to what was quite justly described as wage-slavery. In the reaction from this there was a tendency to swing over and lay all the emphasis upon the other note: community. Value was to be found in the whole society alone, not in its individual members, and this has found in the modern world two main expressions: Communism and Fascism, both of which are totalitarian.

If we are to preserve and develop freedom it must be by maintaining a true balance between the two elements in the divine purpose, which we shall only be able to do in so far as we recognise this purpose as divine—because only the principle of divine love can give security that the welfare of each and the welfare of all is equally a matter of primary concern.

If we are to make progress along this line of true freedom with the recognition that freedom itself is always social and that men and women become persons only through their relationship to one another and to God, we need a new spirit and a new method.

The method must for the most part be the concern of the politicians. Our function is to watch them, spurring them on by a criticism of the existing order in the light of our principles and checking them by criticism of their proposals in the light of our principles.

But the spirit is our own direct concern, and unless there is the spirit of true freedom (that is, concern for persons in community) we shall not in fact adopt the right methods or follow them effectively if we do.

It is hardly necessary to say that the main instrument for developing the new spirit that we need must be sought in education. But that word must receive a wider interpretation than is commonly given to it. It must be taken to cover all the influences that are brought to bear upon the growing character. It works through the home and the school, but the main educator is always society itself, and our concern for the social order is mainly due to its enormous educational power, for good or for ill. No doubt a child born in a really good home, who is entirely happy there and consequently in no way urged to react against it, is likely to develop qualities which the whole influence of society will not pervert, even though it is framed upon principles contrary to those of that home. But we must not expect this to be frequent, for how is the home itself to have that quality if the society all around it has another? In comparison with home and society, the school has relatively small influence. It is of immense importance to secure that this influence is of the right quality, and where it continues or supplements the influence of home, something of supreme value is achieved. But once again, we cannot expect to find the school very much in advance of the society which forms it and surrounds it; we have got to recognise the function of each of these factors in its own place and try to secure that all of them are converging upon our permanent aim—the development of persons in community. Until quite lately the State, as the organ of society, paid no attention to the majority of its young people after fourteen years of age; they were thrown out from school to be members of no community whatever to which they could feel that they belonged or which could seem to belong to them. For the nation—except in time of war—and even the city, is something much too large for any boy or girl to appreciate as genuinely his or her community. And so either each had to fend for himself, which tends to anarchic individualism, or else each had to sink himself in the mass, which tends to the herd-consciousness of Communism.

Here then, as it seems to me, is the point upon which our primary attention should be directed. It is undoubtedly one of the most formative in life, but it might be claimed for others, especially the earlier periods, that they are in themselves more important in that respect.

The reason for our concern about it now is that it has been so grossly neglected. The results of that neglect in other countries have been appalling, and they might well become so in our own if the neglect continues. No doubt the Government has already begun to take action, and had done so just before the war began. During the war, with the Pre-Service Units of various kinds, still more has been done. But the State has not at present shewn at all adequate appreciation of the service of the voluntary agencies in this field, and if the whole passes over to the State, it is almost inevitable that the system will be stereotyped and that we shall be heading for one form or another of totalitarian control.

Therefore we have got to find the way to effect the real marriage of State concern with voluntary enterprise, each welcoming the other and recognising it in its own place. And if we set this problem in the centre of all our thinking, it will give the proper perspective to everything else that we undertake. We are bound to be concerned about housing, about nutrition, about social security, about freedom and unemployment and so forth; but let us be quite clear that our concern with every one of these is dictated and directed by our primary principle—the development of persons in community as children in the family of God. That will cover very nearly every political proposal in the social and economic field. Of course it will not of itself help us to determine what means will be effective to the end that we desire, but it will keep us true as regards our main direction and deliver us, as nothing else can, from the hell that we have made of life by letting the means of our welfare assume in our thought the function and position of that welfare itself.

XX

The Church Looks Forward: V

A SPEECH DELIVERED AT A YOUTH RALLY IN LONDON
ON OCTOBER 3RD, 1943

IT seems only proper that the series of meetings arranged to be addressed by the Archbishop of York and myself together should end with a meeting of young people, because if the principles we have tried to lay down are to be effectively carried out, the task is one that will occupy very many years, and most of its accomplishment must be in the hands of people who are now young.

What do we look for as the special contribution of young people to the life of the Church and the establishment of a more Christian social order? I suppose everyone would agree that we hope especially for two qualities, loyalty and adventure.

Loyalty is the natural expression of the generosity of young folk in face of the fact that their own experience as yet is limited. But this must not mean that their loyalty is primarily to older people who have more experience, but are as likely to have had their imaginations stifled as to have had their wisdom increased by the pressure of that experience. The loyalty of Christian youth must be first and foremost to Christ Himself; and I am sure we make a great mistake if, in our appeal to young people, we ever conceal or put into the back-

142

ground that primary claim. He was Himself still a young man when His earthly ministry ended on the Cross; those whom He gathered about Him were young men who were able, through many years of discipleship, to carry forward the movement He had inaugurated. No one can help this cause who is not first and foremost loyal to Christ as the one leader for all men, and that loyalty must be in the full sense personal. It must express itself not only and not chiefly in trying, by wisdom or strength of our own, to carry out His precepts, but chiefly in the determination to live in constant fellowship with Him and in dependence upon the guidance of His spirit.

Nothing can take the place of the daily time of intimate companionship with the Lord, and that is the first thing to which we would call young Christian people. Make time for it somehow and secure that it is real.

This loyalty to Christ will find expression through active and eager membership of His Church. This again need not and should not imply a passive docility in face of the counsel of elders. The men our Lord chose for His intimate disciples were not at all that type; two of them He nicknamed "Sons of Thunder"; one of them was a Zealot. No doubt their eagerness often led them into mistakes, but He could point out the mistake and train it in a new direction. But He could not make effective use of those who had no energy. We are all familiar with the contrast in the Book of the Acts between the wise and dignified Gamaliel and the hot-headed young Saul of Tarsus. Gamaliel is a great religious teacher, and, confronted with the most searching challenge that ever came to such a man, his advice is to let it alone and see what happens: if God is in the new movement, they cannot resist it; if He is not, it will collapse. So wise! So pious! And so completely lacking in sense of responsibility. It was Gamaliel's plain duty to make up his mind whether the movement was of God or not. Nicodemus had wanted in the same kind of way to help the new movement secretly from his place of vantage in the Sanhedrin, and he was told sharply that he must be ready for a new start if he was even to have a notion what this Kingdom of Heaven is which the movement was all about.

And so we only hear now of Gamaliel because of that one instance of pious futility. But Saul of Tarsus, who breathed out threatenings and slaughter, became the founder of Churches all round the Aegean Sea, the greatest missionary in history and inaugurator of Christian theology.

And so we want people who are ready to make adventure. Some of the adventures will end in disappointment; some of them will bring rebukes from ecclesiastical authorities, middle-aged folk like myself who will be shocked and horrified. Never mind! Sometimes the adventurers will be right and the authorities wrong. But we need men who will seek the guidance of the Spirit of Christ to determine what is right and will then give themselves to it heart and soul; and if, like Saul of Tarsus, they have misunderstood the guidance, their loyalty to what they had believed it to be will secure that fresh illumination will be given.

Adventure and loyalty to Christ is what we want. We want it in men's choice of a career. Nothing depresses me so much as a young man who, when thinking what career he shall take up, begins discussing the prospects of a pension. Be ready to stake yourselves on what you believe is right. And then, even if your career ends in disappointment, there will be something noble even if there is no success.

We want adventure in thought: exercise your minds with freedom and vigour, but still with constant loyalty to Christ.

You will find that loyalty is no fetter, but a most urgent stimulus.

And we want adventure in discipleship: in new ways of expressing our loyalty: in worship and in conduct. Take those two notes: Loyalty and Adventure. Let each interpret the other, and you will do something for the Church of Christ in the coming time and for the civilization which it seeks to influence. If we could have a great multitude of young people forming their vision of the future in loyalty to Christ and then giving themselves heart and soul, in the power of His Spirit, to bring the vision true, there is no limit to what we might accomplish for our country and through it for the world.

XXI

The Christian View of the Right Relationship between Finance, Production and Consumption

A LECTURE TO MEMBERS OF THE BANK OFFICERS' GUILD AT THE CENTRAL HALL, WESTMINSTER, ON THURSDAY, FEBRUARY 4TH, 1943

MY Friends,—I should like to begin, if I may, with a word or two of explanation and almost of apology. The apology, following upon the most eloquent discourse we have just heard, is for being a mere Englishman with the relatively tame manner of speech that befits such; and I am afraid I cannot hope to fire you as you have just been fired. But I am most grateful for the setting in which the Chairman has put our consideration of this matter, because—here is my second point—I was indeed most happy to receive and accept the invitation you kindly sent me; but not particularly because you were a Bank Officers' Guild—I have no special qualification for speaking to Bank Officers—but because I'm glad to speak to any group of people who are ready and willing to listen concerning the place which it seems to me their special occupation holds in the general Christian map of life. That is my concern: to try to see the picture as it must be drawn on Christian principles, and then where the various occupations fit into it, so that those who are engaged in them, if they have the desire—which I may hope they have—to conform their practice to the Christian standard, will see where it still needs modification, where it may need even revolutionary change; or even—very dull but sometimes salutary—where it is already perfectly sound and has only got to be kept going as it is.

It is in that frame of mind, therefore, that I come—not as somebody who has an important pronouncement to make about the way in which business, and especially banking business, should be conducted; but as someone who has tried to think out the view of life as seen in the light of Christian principles and how these three elements in the economic system—finance, production and consumption—must fit together inside it. And therefore I am really more concerned about the words "The Christian View" in my title than I am about anything that follows. I am mainly concerned with the question whether there is a Christian view of these things at all, which I regard as a much more important question than the following one—what the Christian view of them may be. And I find that it is really necessary in these days to persuade people that the Christian Church has quite steadily maintained a witness on these matters, though it has been obscured—never completely obliterated—during the seventeenth and eighteenth centuries, and rather fitfully revived through the nineteenth. I think it's going pretty strong again now.

We begin, of course, with the whole conception of what, on a Christian view, human life is for: Man is created for fellowship in the family of God: fellowship first with God, and through that with all God's other children. And that is the primary test that must be applied to every system that is constructed and every change in the system that is proposed.

Does it help us nearer towards fulness and richness of personal fellowship? And fellowship, of course, is not merely the same thing as all getting together and agreeing with one another: it is compatible with a great deal of disagreement, and with a great deal of variety of experience. If you merely get together like-minded people or people with the same predominant interests in life, you don't get a fellowship; you get a herd, which is a very inferior thing, perfectly familiar in the animal creation. It's great fun belonging to a herd—at any rate when it's hunting or doing something of that sort; but there's nothing morally excellent about it. The herd instinct is no better in itself—or if you like, the gregarious instinct is no better in itself—than the self-regarding instinct; it is capable of good and it is capable of bad; and great masses of human beings have banded themselves together to do the most odious things before now; and the mere fact that a great number of people are united in the pursuit of an object is no sort of reason for supposing that it is a good object or that there is any merit in their union.

Sometimes it becomes important to dwell on that, especially at a moment when we are talking a great deal about democracy; because, of course, there has been a fearful lot of fustian talked about democracy: *vox populi vox dei:* what nonsense! The defence of government by a majority is not that the majority is always right; on the contrary, the only thing you know for certain about a majority with regard to any new issue is that it's sure to be a little wrong. Only you have no earthly means of finding out which of the minorities, if any, is right; and it is very unlikely that the majority will be as wrong as some of the minorities are likely to be. Therefore, it is a great deal safer to let the majority rule than a minority. That's a dull pedestrian argument, isn't it? But, of course, the real defence of democracy is not that at all—it is not in that region. It is that by calling upon people to exercise responsible judgment on the matters before the country at any time, you develop their personal qualities: you make them feel that they belong to one another in this corporate society, and so you tend to deepen and intensify personal fellowship. You are leading people forward from the relationship of the herd to that of real fellowship by the mere process of calling upon them to take their share in the government of the groups of which they are members. That is the real value of the thing, its educational effect upon the citizens, and through that, of course, you get a more alert, a more disciplined intelligence in the citizens—less liable to be swayed by mass hysteria and the like—less likely to be victims of propaganda, one of the subtle perils of democracy at all times—and through that once more you will get, in the long run, a wider and a better government because it is government by wiser and better citizens. But it must always be through that line of argument it seems to me—at least on Christian grounds—that we defend democracy. It is because it gives the highest value, higher than any other political scheme, to the personality and the personal relationships of all the citizens in the community.

Then you go on perhaps to ask, in this fellowship that you are seeking to build up, what are the real points of value, what are the things that confer excellence upon life? And, of course, again, they are always personal qualities and personal relationships. The essence of human life was just as great before they invented the internal combustion engine with all the other things it has made possible. These things can be used no doubt for bringing us into touch with people we should not otherwise have reached, and so increasing our range of contacts and once more the width and depth of our fellowship. They can be used, we know quite well, for perfectly other purposes than those; and the mere multiplication of gadgets, the mere increase of man's power over natural resources, does not of itself constitute progress in any intelligible sense at all: it does not make the world any better. My favourite illustration of that was supplied to me by a Chinese friend of mine speaking to a conference of students in America some seven years ago; all his audience—there were three thousand of them—were people who had just taken their degree or were on the point of taking it, so he opened up like this: "When I took my degree at the University, I was, like everybody else at that time of life, exceedingly foolish". Having so ingratiated himself, he went on: "And the day after I took it, I made a journey from Shanghai, where my University was, into the interior of China which occupied sixteen days. A month or two back I repeated that journey in eighteen hours; but if I am a fool when I get into the aeroplane, I shall still be a fool when I get out of it, and why do you call it progress to distribute my folly about the earth more rapidly?" Well, now, the real goods of life are all in personal qualities and personal relationships: the fulness of personal existence, the width of interest, spiritual, intellectual, imaginative, and the rest, and the relationships with our neighbours, and our friends—these are the things that really constitute the substance of human life, to which everything else ought all the while to be subordinated. And it is very hard, when the apparatus of life, so to speak, begins to be extremely complicated, to maintain that subordination; our business mechanism and our financial mechanism are become so elaborate that those who work them are bound to give an immense amount of time and attention to the mere process of keeping them in order. And that makes it very hard to avoid falling into the error of making these things ends in themselves. They claim so much attention during life that it is very difficult to remember that, after all, their whole value lies in the service they can render to something beyond themselves.

Having got the main standards of value set in that way, I want to justify, if I can, in a very brief outline sketch, my claim that Christianity has quite steadily had a social witness to give. Of course, it starts from the very first days. It is not that they inaugurated any political movement; the first Christians found themselves knit together in so close a fellowship, through the complete supremacy of their faith over their life, that they became an illustration of voluntary communism. None of the disciples said that any of the things he possessed was his own, but they had all things common. It is quite clear that it was voluntary—it was not compulsory: that is made quite plain in the instance where it first began to break down; and a voluntary communism is spiritually very remote from a compulsory communism. There is a great merit if you have some wealth in giving it away. That is an expression of personal character. But to be without any from the beginning is not an expression of personal character at all: it is merely the restriction upon it. And we must therefore always very carefully distinguish in this field the spirit that is permeating the system we are working from the mere mechanism of it. It is possible that a system of compulsory communism would look to the outsider rather like one of voluntary communism. It would be quite different: whether good or bad— different. Well, that was the beginning of it; and they went on, fairly soon, to exercise their minds very much about questions of property, and here you find this interesting fact—

that until the conversion of Constantine, they put forward no suggestions for the ordering of society as a whole. They were unable to influence it : they were a persecuted minority : they were simply dealing with principles for the guidance of their own life within their own little isolated community. But the principles which they laid down at that stage were never recalled, and the first, of course, is this : that the duty of man is to love God with all his heart and his neighbour as himself; nothing short of that is conformity to the will of God : everything short of that therefore is sin.

Now, if we did all love God with all our hearts and our neighbours as ourselves, we should work our hardest to produce what the whole fellowship needed : we should take our own reasonable share of it and no more; and we should be eager that everybody else should have what he needed also, and there would be no need for property rights. And, in consequence, the early theologians are always quite clear that property rights are rooted in sin. They don't say that property is wicked : they say that the whole business is rooted in sin : that is, in the failure of man to rise to the height of his calling, and rights are needed, not for the security of the great property owners, but for the protection of the small property owners : because in a world in which people do not love God with all their hearts, and their neighbours as themselves, the strong are going to take advantage of the weak and you need to protect the weaker members in such rights as they have been able to establish. And then they added to this—but that was rather later—the point that some measure of property is of great value for enabling people to live a free and independent life and express their personality by the direction in which they utilised it, and that, therefore, it was of value because it was useful to the main great concern of developing personality with its opportunities of fellowship. But that sort of thing is as far as they got until the conversion of Constantine: and then Constantine called into the support of his otherwise, at that moment, rather divided and tottering empire this compact and now fairly large—though still a minority—Christian Church, and almost immediately you find them beginning to reflect upon what their duty is, not only within the Christian fellowship itself, but as citizens having an obligation to influence society in the direction that will bring it as near as it can be brought at that moment to conformity with the standards of the Gospel. You find, for example, St. Ambrose dealing with almsgiving—the giving by those who have more than they need for the help of those who have less. Under what heading is it to be classified? Is it mercy? No, it is not; it is justice; and that, of course, is not the way the ordinary person looks at it: he thinks, what I have is my own; if I like to give some of it to somebody else who is badly off, that is a kindness. Well, no doubt, it shows a kindly disposition as distinct from an unkind, hard-hearted one; but these early Christian teachers would have said: "Yes, that may be so, but essentially it is a mere act of justice; it is not anything which has merit in it over and above justice, because justice requires that the strong should help the weak, if you are approaching the matter from the Christian end at all". Then, under the influence of thoughts like that, and the steadily strengthening influence also of the great philosophers, Plato through St. Augustine, and, later on—a good deal later on—Aristotle through St. Thomas—you've got the great medieval system built up, and it would plainly take much too long to describe it at all in detail, nor do I know that I am competent to do that—but it had certain main principles which I believe to be of permanent importance. The two pillars of the Christian system of economics in the Middle Ages were the prohibition of usury and the doctrine of the just price. They had great difficulty in determining what usury was. There always has been great difficulty about that. They were quite clear that usury was always wrong, but they were not equally clear whether this particular transaction is usurious, and that is a much more difficult matter. But let us first notice that they had got behind them on this question of usury an enormous weight of authority, because the total prohibition of it occurs both in Moses and in Aristotle, and that is a very strong combination.

The discussion: *What does constitute usury?* has bothered the Church perpetually. I wish it were bothering us now, because it is that kind of mental trouble which stimulates the public conscience. You can focus attention upon a principle when there is public debate how it ought to be applied far better than if there is no such debate; and, if we could start discussing what kind of loans ought to be regarded as usurious and therefore immoral, it would, I think, help us a long way forward. But the principle behind it is perfectly clear. The principle is twofold: first, one which the Chairman has already mentioned: money is in its own nature a medium of exchange, and, therefore, if you use it as a commodity in the sense of trying to profit yourself by variations in its value over against goods, you are destroying it for its proper social purpose; and there are some kinds of activity in that direction which I think public opinion is tending to think ought undoubtedly to be prohibited, as for example, speculation in foreign currencies. This is not a crime of the Banks, which never, I believe, indulge in this evil practice. It is a crime of the private fortune-hunter. If it can be stopped, it ought to be stopped. I don't think anybody disputes that it has done a vast amount of harm and created a great deal of suffering. It is extremely difficult to prohibit any of the internal and domestic uses of money as a commodity, and I certainly am not going to suggest how it could be done; but the principle that money should function as a means of exchange, and that those who have the handling of it should receive no doubt a perfectly reasonable remuneration for their integrity and their honesty in dealing with it, but not have the opportunity by that mere manipulation of creating new values for themselves which do not correspond to any useful services offered by them to the community—that is, I think, an undoubtedly sound principle.

At what point you should begin to apply such principles, as I have said, the Church was constantly in difficulty; and it was perpetually revising its schemes about this in order to keep pace, so to speak, with the developments in the actual industrial and commercial worlds, so that its main principles should be continually applied, even to the kinds of transaction which had not been in the least contemplated when the first formulations were drawn up; and that went on pretty steadily down to the middle of the fifteenth century. There was, of course, we all know, a great spiritual slump in the fifteenth century; it had been beginning before, but spiritual life was then at a low ebb, and many of the older institutions were failing to discharge their functions as they had done; perhaps they were no longer in gear with society as it was developing. And so before the Reformation came, the Church was already losing its power of moral witness in these matters. The Reformers tried hard to revive it, but the turmoil of the time was so great that they could do very little more than make some adjustments or merely reiterate the old principles in accordance with their own experience of life. Luther, for example, was a peasant, and in this field remained a complete conservative, content to repeat the prohibition of usury, and the doctrine of the just price, of which I will say something in a minute.

Calvin was a citizen of one of the newly developing, very flourishing centres of commerce, and tried to bring to bear the old principles upon that new situation, with the result that one of his followers said of him that Calvin dispensed usury as an apothecary doth poison. That is to say, he regarded it as something which might be administered, so to speak, in minute doses. What he was really doing, of course, was to find the just way of applying the old principle to the altered conditions; but he was not followed; as far as I know—none of the leading Puritan divines followed it up on the Continent or here. That may be due to gaps in my knowledge, but I don't think it was followed up, and so on this whole field there was a cessation of effective witness through the seventeenth and eighteenth centuries.

The doctrine of the just price was that you are entitled to charge, for what you sell, what covers the cost to you plus a reasonable return as estimated by the current habit of society, and the kind of position that society was expecting you to maintain. In those days, society had a fairly rigid structure—it was not so fluid as we are now, it was a society more of status than of contract as the phrase used to be; and one of the questions that we have got to ask ourselves in these modern times is how far our grandfathers were quite right when they regarded it as sheer gain that we should have moved from the basis of status to a basis of contract. It is quite true that in the early Middle Ages the serf had very great restrictions upon his freedom; he was not in any full sense a free man; but he had some rights and he had security. There was no chance of his falling through the bottom; he had his recognised place in society, and society cared for him in that place.

You remove the basis of status and put everybody on the basis of free contract and free competition, there is much more freedom, people can try and forge their own way ahead. There will be initiative, enterprise, expansion of all sorts— yes—and also there may be people who will fall out at the bottom; and we are having deliberately to rebuild that basic foundation of society so that the people may not fall through, so to speak.

No doubt we have always recognised an obligation to save people from literal physical starvation; even the Poor Law of 1834 recognised that, but subject to such restrictions upon personal liberty as made it—as we know—to stink in the nostrils of people who were primarily concerned in it. And now first with the Unemployment Benefit introduced after the last war, now with steady development of all that, and in the future with something that will carry out, as we hope, the principles of the Beveridge Report, we are deliberately rebuilding the basis which was once supplied to society by the principle of status, putting it in as it were as a kind of under-pinning to the structure of freedom of contract resting upon it. But, of course, you can't do it without much modifying all that system of freedom of contract, I think modifying it in beneficial ways, but it will be very profoundly changed in the process.

Well, that is then what the just price meant; you see, it is a complete condemnation of the belief that the price of goods should be regulated primarily by the law of supply and demand. That is the main difference between medieval and nineteenth-century economics; we have come almost to take it for granted, as a law of nature, that the price of things is governed by this law of supply and demand; but you know it is not. At the beginning of the last war, I had a letter from my tailor, who was a good Christian man and who said, "You will have noticed that the price of cloth has very largely risen lately, owing to war shortage, but I should like you and my other customers to know that I happen to have bought a little while before the war a very large stock of cloth and I shall, of course, supply my customers as long as it shall last at the original figures and not take advantage of this general rise". Well, I hope it was good business for him; I think it very likely was, because many of us were the more eager to go to him out of self-regarding motives and also out of respect for him. So, as I say, I hope it was good business, but he certainly did it because he felt that it would be immoral for him merely to pocket the difference on the ground that people would be ready to pay it.

The law of supply and demand is a non-moral law. It is not exactly immoral. It just has nothing to do with morals, and, of course, it is also true that you cannot go on selling a thing indefinitely at a loss or you go out of business. Of course you do. All these things are the normal and non-moral mechanical structure; but what we have allowed to happen to so vast an extent is to let this non-moral mechanical structure become the sole determinant of our conduct, and we have got to find our way back to use that machine, as we have got to find the way back to use the internal combustion engine itself, in the interests of human fellowship and the richness of human personality.

Well, then, we come to the actual question in the title; as the Chairman has already said, production exists for consumption, and if you treat it otherwise, things will begin to go wrong. You see, all industrial production always is co-operation for the public service, in itself, not necessarily in the minds of the people who are doing it. In itself, it consists in the actual co-operation of a vast number of people; people who grow the raw materials, people who carry them across the seas, and people who work them up in all the different processes, and along with that the skill of the manager, and the finance of the capitalist by which the whole process is made possible at the outset. And all of them are co-operating whether they know it or not, and whether they want to be or not, they are. And it goes on in the end of the day for public service because, if the public do not want what is produced, no more happens. You can do a good deal by advertisement to make people buy what they won't want, but whether it is a moral process, again I don't know. But let us remember that it was the experience of commercial advertisement that taught the secret of the thing to Goebbels for political adver-tisement, and there would never have been that type of politi-cal propaganda if people hadn't found out the psychological weaknesses that can be played on by skilful advertising. But evidently production does exist for the consumer, and if the consumer just won't buy it, again the process stops, and some people are prepared to accept that and say, "Yes, but as it always is in the consumer's interest, what are you troubling about?" Yes, but what I want is that it should be plainly and consciously directed to the consumer's interest; no doubt it often is, but, quite equally, no doubt it may not be, and you may have cases where, as the Chairman has suggested already, there is a deliberate checking of some new process that would be immensely to the public advantage, in order to maintain the price ring for the productive concerns that are already in the field.

But do not let us swing over at once and say that the proper thing to do is always to bring in the new thing and let the public get the benefit, because part of the public is the people engaged in those productive concerns, and when you bring the new process in you may throw them all out of work and do great damage that way. What is wanted is, of course, as usual, the whole view, the look all round, which remembers that producers themselves are in their turn consumers, and therefore, while production is for consumption, it is not true that producers exist for consumers. They are human beings, ends in themselves as much as anybody else, and the whole process must be so adjusted that in the very process of production they are able to the utmost possible extent to realise their personality and their fellowship. And so you have always got a double thing to consider at once—it is very difficult—both the wider fellowship in which the producer is related to another consumer, and the narrower one within the productive process where you want to see the same ideal human relationships reproduced so far as ever circumstances permit. There has never been the prospect, at least not for a very long time, to do it quite perfectly, but that is no reason for not getting as close towards it as you can.

And finance—quite plainly—exists to facilitate the production which exists in the interests of consumption, and finance again has its own undeniable rights. It could not be proper for those who are administering it to risk money that has been entrusted to them by the public in unsound ventures, or in allowing business which at first seemed to be sound actually to absorb and destroy those savings without any kind of security or return. On the other hand, finance very easily gets into the position, and needs to be constantly vigilant against getting into the position, of a positive control on the productive machine; for that it is not qualified. I am not sure what the theological moralists would have said about systems of mortgaging and the like, but they would have been very shy of them. Perhaps it is the only way in the modern world in which the necessary—quite necessary—security can be obtained; but there is something always rather anxious about it, because, as I have said, behind all these Christian principles there always lay the primary demand that on no account should the stronger exploit the weaker. Now if a man is engaged in an enterprise in which he has borrowed money on the security of his plant, and he then does in fact fail to make a success of it, very likely the lenders—or those who have acted for the lenders, who in the last resort are always the public itself, or some portion of it—must be guaranteed something in return; but if what is taken over in return is the whole plant, so that the man who has undertaken the business is simply turned out of it, it very likely means that it comes into the hands of people who have no enthusiasm for it, and its nominal value very quickly disappears. So that, on the economic ground alone, it may not be profitable, but on the moral ground it is at least an extraordinarily dangerous method which wants constant vigilance lest it be applied in a tyrannous manner. I think this has happened in other countries, if not in our own.

The mere economic consideration of life tends to ignore human personality and human fellowship; of course, it cannot help it; it is not concerned with those things; it is concerned with the mechanism of supply to keep people alive while they develop their personality and their fellowships; and as I have already said, it is so intricate and so exacting that those engaged in it very easily lose sight of the thing that it exists to serve. Then, when that happens, your financial or economic pressures tend to be a real solvent and a dissolvent of all that is most valuable in society. There has lately been put forward, I am told, in the United States a proposal which, again I am told, has gained some support from this side of the Atlantic, for the institution of a world bank which is designed, broadly speaking, to control the credit of the world universally. As far as I know, it will be responsible to nobody, and I do not see who there is to whom it could possibly be responsible; we have not got, and are plainly not going to have for a long time, anything like a world Government; so that you would have an enormous instance of irresponsible power. Its economic convenience I see perfectly well, but if you regard it as axiomatic that irresponsible power is always an evil, you will be very shy of this expedient coming in at this stage of human history. No doubt there is need for an international clearance system like the Bank for International Settlement, but we must be very shy of a World Bank with control of the credit of all nations.

But, further, I am assured that this scheme contemplates an absolute fluidity of labour, so that people may be transferred not only from one part of their own country to another, but from their own country to another country according to the state of the market and the best opportunities of production. Now that means that you are treating human beings primarily as instruments of production; that is simply immoral. It means that you would be ready to sacrifice richness of human personality, all the fellowships, all the traditions that grow up in the localities to which people belong; all these loyalties that do so much to enrich life and give it its strength and its colour would be subordinated to the sheer demand of maximum economic output and maximum ease of distribution. Now efficiency of output is of very great importance, effective distribution is of very great importance, but they are important for the sake of something beyond themselves. They are important for the sake of human life, with all its qualities, and whatever restrictions may be put upon economic development by the elementary requirements of human life have got to be accepted.

That is the fundamental principle, as I see it, in the Christian view of the relation of these three things to one another. It is not within themselves that Christianity has anything to say about it, but in the whole setting of life which Christianity gives you, which requires you then to adjust these to one another in such a way as to fulfil their part in the whole scheme. I have only one more thing I should wish to say about it, and that is that I do not see the smallest prospect of those principles being effectively applied unless there is at least a large body of people who find the inspiration for their application in a faith which is something much more than the hope of a terrestrial Utopia. By all means let us welcome whole-heartedly the help of those who have not got the priceless privilege of a faith rooted in something beyond this world. Let us co-operate with them to the full in doing that which they and we agree is desirable to be done. Let us also be quite clear about the special responsibility which rests upon those who have got that faith to see that it becomes effective in these spheres; and, if we hold this view, let us not—those of us who have that position—be backward in warning others of the risk that the self-interest that is so deep in everyone of us will break out again and spoil the whole enterprise, however idealistic in its first conception, unless that self-interest is counteracted by a Power other than the mere exercise of human volition—the power of the Spirit of God in the hearts of those who are open to it. For I at least am quite sure of this, that we shall never achieve the purpose about which we were singing a moment ago, of building Jerusalem in England's green and pleasant land, unless we are first and foremost citizens of that Jerusalem which is above and free and is the mother of us all.

XXII

The Spirit of Management

AN ADDRESS DELIVERED TO THE INSTITUTE OF INDUSTRIAL
MANAGEMENT ON MARCH 6TH, 1943

IT is probably true of industry, as of so much else in national
life, that the effect of war is immensely to accelerate what has
already been in progress. Certainly the war has brought to the
fore the vital importance of Management. But already before
the war, many observers were ready to say that Management
rather than Ownership was the key-point for those who were
concerned with the welfare of industry alike in its inner organisation and in its relationship to the community.

At an earlier date Ownership and Management were very
closely connected, and this remains true over a large part of
industry, especially that large section within which the number of men employed by a single firm is comparatively small.
But it is evident that the presence of managerial capacity in
the owners of capital (whether the latter takes the form of
shares or of actual plant) is accidental. This was a source of
comparatively little damage in the early days of industrial
development: a man who had the opportunity would start a
small factory; if he had the requisite ability he made a success of it and it developed, possibly into something very large;
if he had not the ability, it failed; he went back to the ranks
of the wage-earners, and before very long, in those days of
steady expansion, his employees found work elsewhere. At

that time the quality vital for development was initiative, and though the morals of the situation were those of the jungle, the expansion of industry went forward on this basis more rapidly than it probably could have done on any other; and it was at least arguable that this was what would most conduce to the welfare of the country.

But these principles cannot be applied without intolerable evils to the great concerns with which we are now familiar. The interest of the community itself in the products of these great undertakings is very great. The number of persons employed in them is immense. Consequently any risk of failure through inefficiency is a social evil too great to contemplate. And in response to this new situation there has been arising as a new factor the whole class of Managers, who are not themselves Owners or members of owning families, but are qualified by their own talents, by their training and experience, for the exercise of what is now far the most responsible task in relation to industry and its service to the community.

With the rise of the professional Manager, the Owner as such inevitably withdraws into the background. As regards the very big concerns, which must be uppermost in our minds, the Owners are the shareholders, who in fact exercise no control upon the conduct of the business at all. They cannot know enough about it. As a rule they are not organised, and therefore could not give effect to their wishes if they had any. Forty years ago the Christian Social Union used to urge its members if they held any shares to attend shareholders' meetings and raise the demand for improved conditions for the workers. The aim was right, because ownership ought always to be associated with responsibility; but the method was impracticable. Now the Owners do not as a rule seek directly to influence the course of business. Board of Directors, though nominally elected by the Owners, are in practice very largely co-optive, and their supreme responsibility is to find, whether from among themselves or from outside, the best Manager, to whom thereafter the main responsibility belongs.

What is the professional interest of this new and immensely important section of the community? It certainly ought to be —but also, I believe, it nearly always is—*efficiency of service to the community.* Perhaps of those three terms the emphasis is laid on each in a dwindling scale: The main concern is efficiency of actual working; yet it is efficiency in providing the community with its needs and therefore it is of service; and this service is rendered to the community as a whole, though perhaps that is not often vividly present to consciousness, except during a war.

Undoubtedly the interest of the Managers is not identical with the financial interest of the Owners. They are not concerned primarily with producing the largest dividends, though they are interested in profits as a means of measuring efficiency. To me it appears that this outlook of the profession of Management is entirely to be welcomed, and so far as there is conflict between this natural interest of the Manager and his technical obligation to do the best he can for the Owner, encouragement should be given to his natural bent. In all personal interest he stands with all others who are carrying on the work rather than with those who hope to derive from it a return on their capital invested in it. And so with the emergence of the Manager into the foremost place, the motive of profit-seeking, in the sense of personal advantage, goes into the second place, as compared with efficiency of service.

As with all human things, there are some accompanying risks. Probably everyone here has read Mr. Burnham's book *The Managerial Revolution.* Mr. Burnham tells us that he was once a Trotskyist, and I am quite sure that no one who is capable of being a Trotskyist, even for a short time, or indeed of being any other kind of doctrinaire Communist, is also capable of estimating at all accurately the trends and tendencies of English life. But though in this book one tendency is isolated and presented as if it were the whole key to the future, there is no doubt about the importance of that tendency as one of the factors contributing to our future social order. And the danger of the exaltation of the Manager is of course what is commonly described as bureaucracy. It is better than plutocracy, and it is better than mob government; but it may easily be the enemy of that development of responsible citizenship which is the essence of true democracy. There is no need why it must be so, and if Managers are really sensitive to the human interests of those who work in the business which they control, the danger will be avoided. But if that is to happen, the recruitment and training of Managers becomes of paramount importance. The two cannot well be separated, because there will be need to look out for men of leadership in all ranks of those employed, while there will be need also to send through all the departments of the business those who, on grounds of personal talent, are selected from elsewhere for training as future Managers.

But the question of general education here assumes a great importance. No doubt the Manager should be acquainted with the workings of all the machinery which the men under his control have to operate. But it is still more important that he should understand the men themselves. At least one great "captain of industry" in the last age—Mr. Lionel Hichens—steadily maintained that for the higher posts of Management he always wanted men who had taken Greats at Oxford—that is to say, men who had studied history and philosphy, because what he wanted in them first was trained minds, sensitive to human feelings and aspirations. It seems to me that we have tended to leave that vital element too much out of sight. We have tended to assume that while it requires careful training to manipulate a complicated engine, no training at all is required to enable a man to manipulate a whole team of human beings. But leadership can be developed by appropriate training, even if the seeds of it must be inborn if they are to be present at all. And that training comes partly through living together in a community such as a boarding school or residential University provides, partly through the exercise of the mind upon human aspirations and endeavours. Of course the technical qualifications are necessary; my plea is that they are no more necessary than the human qualifications, and that the higher you go in the ranks of Management, the more vitally important do the human qualifications become.

Management, then, in the days that are before us will be the vital link between industry and the community, because upon it will depend the happiness and contentment of the great army of those employed in industry, and upon it will also depend the guidance of industry in the ways that will most intimately affect the community for its weal or its woe.

XXIII

Britain and Germany after the War

AN ADDRESS DELIVERED IN THE CHURCH
OF ST. JUDE ON THE HILL ON OCTOBER 18TH, 1942

> Think not that I came to destroy the law of the prophets,
> I came not to destroy but to fulfil.
>
> *Matthew* v. 17

THERE has been delivered here a series of discourses under the title "The Voice of the Laity", and it is in association with that series, though hardly as one able to speak with that voice, that I am allowed to say something to you this evening on a subject that was suggested to me, not chosen by me, entitled "Britain and Germany after the War", which means, of course, for Christians, simply the question of how after such a conflict a Christian community should treat its enemies. And if we are to answer that question we must go behind the present crisis and consider the permanent rules for our guidance which are to be found in our faith.

The Christian religion is, among other things, a philosophy of history. It contains an account of how it has come to pass that in a world that God made there should be such horrors as those we have witnessed. This is due to man's rebellion. God has a law for man that he should love God with all his heart and his neighbour as himself, and everything other than that is sin, for it is contrary to the will and law of God. Do let us remember that this is what the Christian

170

Church always means, and what Christian people ought to mean, by the word "Sin". Sin is anything less than love of God and of our neighbour as ourselves.

And we have not kept that law. There are few men who have kept it even for a short period of their lives. There is none who has kept it throughout the whole of life. And when we pass from individuals to those great groupings of men which are always more self-centred than the individuals that compose them, we are very far from obedience to that law.

Take a crucial instance from the present conflict. If the Germans and Poles had loved each other as themselves in the summer of 1939 there would have been no war. There might have been considerable time spent in the adjustment of what was indeed an extremely difficult situation, while in friendship the representatives of the two sides met together to think out how justice could really be done to the different cultures and traditions which had become so intermixed in that region. But there would have been no fighting.

We may trace it back through the history leading to any war and through all the history of all mankind, and we can see quite easily, when we stop to think for a moment, that nearly everything that embitters life can be removed from it if we live up to these two great commandments. But we do not, and what is more, we cannot. It is no good saying that we should love God with all our hearts—we do not know enough about Him; and your neighbour as yourself, for he will irritate you just as much to-morrow as he did to-day. You cannot suddenly evolve from within yourself the reserve of love which would enable you to accept that irritation, or something more than irritation, from your neighbour, and by enduring whatever it may be, make his fault the occasion of a better love between you. That is the Christian way, but we cannot follow it except in the power of God that grows in our heart, if we find the companionship of Him in whom alone it is possible—Jesus, perfect God and perfect Man.

The Christian religion gives us also the direction of progress and gives us the standard by which to test every new movement and to judge whether it is real progress or not. And the standard is simply this—does it set forward love and goodwill amongst men or is it a new expression of self-assertion, pride, greed and domination? Whatever sets forward true love among men is progress. Whatever hinders it is movement in the wrong way. The greatest delusion that can possibly seize upon the human mind is the supposition that whatever happens next is bound to be better. We really might have learnt that by now, but it seems many of us have not.

The Christian religion gives us no assurance that there will ever be upon this earth a society of perfect love, indeed it gives us many reasons to believe there never will be, but it is a matter of small consequence whether the divine purpose to sum up all things in Christ be fulfilled on this planet or not. Certainly it cannot be completely fulfilled on this planet, because there will always be born into this world new finite spirits who take themselves to be the centre of the world and so upset all the harmony again—and that is the essence of sin —and partly also because the fellowship we have been taught to look forward to is one that must include all the generations of mankind, which in our mortal state is plainly impossible.

The Christian religion, then, accounts for our unhappy state, gives the test and direction of progress and supplies the stimulus we need. The inspiration to progress towards the more perfect realisation of love is the governing force of human life through the revelation of the Divine Love in the Life, Death, Resurrection and Teaching of Christ. And it indicates to us also the method of progression, which is that we seek to come to all our tasks and duties and also to all amusements as from His presence, and bearing with us His presence to control us.

But as we pass from stage to stage there are always two instruments by which God guides us—the law and the Gospel. We must not set these against one another as though they contradicted one another. Christ did not come to destroy the law, but to fulfil or complete it. In the divine method of preparing the world for Him the law had its place, and only when a certain standard of conduct has been established and man's selfish desires and ambitions are to some extent controlled under the influence of the law and its sanctions does the Gospel come which leads us to heights beyond anything to which the law could ever call us, to a life of love which requires no sanctions.

The Christian life in practice always consists of a difficult balance between these elements. The familiar instance of this is, of course, the contrast between the Christian and the Pharisee. It is quite easy to be a genial libertine—friendly with everyone you meet, if you have for yourself and them no moral standard. And it is fairly easy for you to set up a moral standard for yourself and others—no doubt underlining the words *"for others"*—if you allow yourself in the process to become hypercritical, unsympathetic and censorious, which is to be a Pharisee. But to set up a standard for others and yourself—with the words *"for yourself"* underlined—and still show sympathy and love to those who fail to reach it, without letting the standard down, that is very hard. But that is to be a Christian.

That is the familiar and significant instance of the difficulty in balancing two things which taken separately would be easy to realise, but which in combination are very hard—so hard that only in the fellowship of Christ and in the power of His Spirit shall we get very far in doing this. And it is so with the principles of the law and the Gospel, which must both be in our minds if we are to make our contribution as Christian people to the right settlement of the world when the war is over, and especially with those who in the war are our enemies.

Let us remember that when we pass from the realm of pure principle to the realm of action it is our duty as Christians to think out that kind of action which is practicable in the world we know with such human nature as ours and that of our neighbours as its agent; not to dream of what would be a perfect world if everyone already were a perfect Christian. Even then if we should be successful in establishing it for a moment we should break it to pieces in a fortnight. No, we have not reached the stage in which we can hope to live by the Gospel only, with no reference to the law.

You and I still need the law in our private lives to strengthen us in our weaker moments. It was a Master of Balliol who said: "Personally, I *prefer* to purchase my railway ticket, but doubtless the presence of a ticket inspector has often clinched the matter!" The law which upholds our purpose to lead an honest life is not a limitation of our freedom, but rather the support and stay of it. Freedom is not shown in the following of desires which arise in our minds at any moment, for that is sheer slavery. That is the bondage of sin. Freedom is shown in the pursuit of the purpose which is sufficiently great to claim our service throughout our lives. It is a matter not of the desires, but of the will—the power of forming a purpose by which to give to each part of life its own place in the economy of the whole.

And so we have to consider what is the kind of action and what are the principles that guide us, knowing that we shall not have, after the war, upon either side, nations composed of saints! And I have no hesitation in saying that after such events as we have witnessed, the first post-war need is the expression of justice.

Let us pause for a moment to remind ourselves that justice is the first expression of love. It is not something contrary to love, which love mitigates and softens. It is the first expression of it that must be satisfied, before the other and higher expressions can rightly find their places.

You think, for example, of how you should apply the principle of love in industrial disputes. How are the Trades Union Committee to express it in dealing with the Employers' Federation? Is it their first duty to consider the employers' interests, and only afterwards to attend to the interests of the men they represent? That is nonsense. The Committee who took that course would merit instant dismissal. The only apparent way in which love can be shown is by meting out justice. Let each side state its case as strongly as it can be stated with perfect fairness before the most impartial tribunal that can be established, with full determination to accept the award. That places your neighbour's interests and your own upon a level; and that is the first thing to be done in "loving your neighbour as yourself".

Justice, then, with all its requirements, is not something alien from love; it is its true expression, and the necessary first stage of its complete expression. But justice is inevitably stern. It refuses merely to overlook wrongs that have been done. God, in Christ, does not overlook wrongs that have been done, but takes them into Himself. And perhaps, if you thought we really had the spiritual power to take these evils unto ourselves, and so negate them by meeting them with perfect love, that might be the right way to treat them. But we cannot do it. If we dream of that we deceive ourselves, and the result, in fact, will be something very different; it will be a condoning of the evil, and that is worse than all.

So justice inevitably involves penalties, and these in two forms. There must first be punishment of individuals proved guilty of proved atrocities. But let us try to be sure we mean business by the word "proved". No doubt proof in anything like a mathematical sense is impossible. It always is impossible in any court of law. But we all know the conditions which lead to the establishment of guilt. There must be opportunity for defence, and there must be the greatest attainable impartiality in judging—a very difficult requirement, but a requirement which is indispensable if the penal action is going to produce upon the future generations the moral effect for the sake of which it is taken. So the punishment must be imposed by a judicial procedure calculated as far as may be to satisfy all concerned that the cases are really proved, and that those who suffer are really guilty.

And secondly, apart from the punishment of individuals, there is the need to express justice as between the nations. We have witnessed an outbreak in Europe three times over from one nation. It must be made clear to that nation, as also to others, that such conduct is intolerable, and will for the future be rendered impossible. But here a special difficulty confronts us, because so far as any settlement is penal it loses its quality of justice as the years pass. No penal settlement can be both just and permanent, for you must not personify a nation and treat it as though it were a single moral agent. It consists of a multitude of individuals, and these are grouped in successive generations; and if a generation grows up under restrictions imposed for what were the acts of its predecessors it will be embittered, and have a real grievance against that settlement, and a moral ground for seeking every opportunity to overthrow it.

So there is need for both a short-term and a long-term treatment. There ought to be such expression of moral condemnation of recent German policy as cannot fail to bring home to the people of that land what is the moral judgment of the world concerning them. On the other hand, there must be in the long-term policy provision that the coming generation shall be able to recognise the position given them in the world as a fair one.

Then there must be—much more difficult—the task of education. When we study the history of nations we shall be slow to suggest that any one nation has violence and aggressiveness in its blood in any predominant degree. But we are bound to take note of the situation in our own times. We must remember that in previous ages it was not Germany, but France, who sought to dominate Europe, and against whom our nation fought to prevent that domination. We were guided, as I suggest most nations always have been, by a mixture of moral and selfish considerations. It was certainly contrary to our interests as an island off the coast of the European continent that any one power should dominate there. And we have steadily resisted such domination, and have always represented that resistance as being not only in the interests of ourselves, but also of those nations who were to be the subjects of such domination. What we notice is the moral aspect of our action, while our neighbours notice that it suited our own interests very well. They attend to the one, we to the other.

But France is not the source of danger now; such a danger has come from Germany three times in one long lifetime, and therefore it is with that nation that the politicians must be concerned. But they must be concerned with it on the ground of general principle—the principle of trying to secure that all kinds of violent aggression shall be made impossible. The fact that it is directed for the moment against one group does not invalidate the general principle.

With that there must come the training of a new mentality. This is very difficult. Who is to do it? We are, of course, assuming in all this something of which we need have no doubt, that we shall have won the war, and that the settlement will in some measure be in our hands. And we are thinking of the influence we are to bring to bear. It will not be possible for *us* to do very much in the way of creating a new mentality in the German people. No vanquished nation will accept such education from its conquerors. We must put that out of our thoughts. I set great hopes upon those people in Germany who through this time have been suffering bravely and constantly for the truth, persecuted and oppressed, and who will be recognised afterwards as having alone been loyal to what would have saved their nation from disaster. They will be able to do much.

We may perhaps consider how we are to influence the teaching of history which takes so great a part in shaping our international outlook. The present regime in Germany has quite deliberately re-written history to make it propaganda for their own interpretation of Germany's destiny. We have never done anything so gross as that, though our reading and teaching of history has not been free from nationalist propaganda. I am speaking of what is some years old; I remember how they told me a great deal about Crecy and Agincourt, and how I heard that young Henry VI was crowned King of France. I often wondered why Calais was all that was left to be written upon Queen Mary's heart. Then one day I came across a French history book which briefly referred to Agincourt as "an engagement"; then followed page upon page of victorious campaigns in which the English had been driven off the soil of France.

We do not want an alien propaganda, we want the truth. You cannot teach history in all its completeness; you have to exercise some selection. But in this our influence must be steadily thrown in favour of such selection as will preserve the proportion and perspective of truth.

I have heard from a Continental scholar the suggestion that a new international authority should require in all countries the study of history from Swiss textbooks, which are very scholarly and written from the point of view of an age-long neutrality. It would be a good thing for all of us.

But by some means or other we must correct the nationalist trend in all our training of the rising generation, and particularly in Germany, where what we call the Prussian tradition has become so strong.

But Christians, at any rate, and civilised men generally, cannot be content to treat one great member of the human family, of the family of nations, as quite distinct from all the others, and merely standing over against them. There might be need for a period of that treatment in what we may call the short-term policy; but we must look beyond that to renewed fellowship; and while the settlement is bound to be such as will appear severe to the German State, we must take care that the long-term settlement secure for the ordinary German citizen of future generations an even chance of sharing in the benefits of civilisation, provided his State is behaving as a good neighbour.

And beyond all that, we shall need all the cultural ties and associations that are possible to build up again mutual understanding. And especially we must try to strengthen all those means of fellowship which unite the Christians of Germany with their fellow Christians in other countries.

And here, in the judgment of Christians at least, must be the one real hope of a fellowship deep and strong enough to resist all tendencies towards division. Around us now the fellowship of Christians is sufficient reality to give us a basis for that hope. There are gathered in this church representatives of very many nations and Christian communions, all joining wholeheartedly in the worship of the One God whom we know and adore through the One Lord and in the power of the One Spirit. And there has been growing up in this last period a new Christian fellowship, little known, alas, to many members of the Christian Churches in our land, but steadily becoming stronger and more able to exercise a very real influence. I would ask you to try to become aware of what is called the "Oecumenical Movement", which finds its expression in great world conferences such as that held in Amsterdam as late as July 1939, at which there were gathered together representatives of more nations than ever the League of Nations could assemble. There was only one name in which they could have been brought together, and that was in the name of Our Lord Jesus Christ. And whatever differences there may have been between them, they recognised their common bond of faith. There is our greatest hope.

At the close of this service we shall be dedicating a memorial to one whose life was given in the service of children being evacuated from this country. I knew something of him, and I know how well he deserves the honour that will be paid him to-day. But let us remember that in all nations in this time of testing there are those who have shown that same capacity for devotion and have recognised that the source of any sacrifice of themselves that they could make was the love of God in Christ. In this great multitude who have passed on we have a silent witness and a constant inspiration. They are one with us in the Communion of Saints. We, if we truly lift up our hearts to the Lord and find that we are not alone with Him, but are in the company of Angels and Archangels and all the whole company of heaven, may find in that Communion of all the Saints which overleaps all divisions and blots out all the bitterness of human strife, a bond of unity which may enable us to do something of great moment towards healing the wounds of the world.

XXIV

Babel and Pentecost

A SERMON PREACHED AT THE OECUMENICAL SERVICE HELD
IN WESTMINSTER ABBEY ON WHITSUNDAY,
JUNE 13TH, 1943

> And the Lord said, Behold they are one people and they
> have all one language; and this is what they begin to do, and
> now nothing will be withholden from them which they pur-
> pose to do. Go to, let us go down and there confound their
> language that they may not understand one another's speech.
>
> *Genesis* xi. 6, 7

> We do hear them speaking in our tongues the wonderful
> works of God.
>
> *Acts* ii. 11

THE Bible opens with a series of stories each of which has
the same moral; that moral is that whenever men acquire
new knowledge, new pleasure, new power, they first make a
selfish and therefore a bad use of it. The series culminates in
the discovery of the art of building with its new gift of security against the powers of nature, with resultant independence
of God and usurpation of the place of God.

This so far presents a bitterly exact correspondence with
the facts of history and of experience. For illustration let us
recall the miseries of the early factories when water-power and
then steam-power was first applied to manufacture—the ex-
ploitation of the weak by the strong, the hideous hours and
conditions of labour for women and children, and all the rest
of the sorry tale set out in such a book as *The Town Labourer*.

And think once more of the use which men have made of aviation. Here is a glorious conquest won by man through science; and its chief use hitherto has been to add to the other horrors of war the bombing of cities with its inevitable accompaniment of indiscriminate slaughter. Every new boon man first degrades into a curse; everything that should make for wider and richer fellowship he makes into a cause of fresh and bitterer division. The things which should have been for our wealth become to us an occasion of falling. That is the state of fallen men.

The supreme usurpation is spoken of as frustrated by the confusion of men's speech. The ambition of Babel—to build a tower by which man should ascend to the throne of God—led to that name becoming a synonym for confusion. For man could achieve even the semblance of success in his Titanic self-assertion only if he could prevent the outbreak of divisions and rivalries. The multiplication of tongues, each representing a special tradition and a peculiar hope, has effectively prevented man from achieving a godless contentment. Thus from the selfish ambition which essays the blasphemous task of establishing an independence of God and usurpation of His throne springs also the selfish rivalry which makes the effort ineffectual. Evil has at least this much of good about it that its own nature renders it self-destructive.

One chief effect of the gift of the Holy Spirit is the reversal of the curse of Babel. Whatever their birthplace with its own language and tradition, men hear the messengers of the Gospel speaking in their own tongue the wonderful works of God. This is one way of saying that the effect of the presence of the Holy Spirit within and among men is always Fellowship: or again, that the word of the Gospel is the word of reconciliation.

The state of nature for man apart from God has much about it which is noble, generous and beautiful; but all is so infected with pride and selfishness that the predominant factor is rivalry and enmity—if not between individuals, then between families, or classes, or nations. Hobbes' phrase is no doubt an exaggeration, but is not worse than a caricature of the truth: in the state of nature the life of man is "solitary, poor, nasty, brutish and short". The state of man as he may be under the guidance of the Holy Spirit and the direction of divine grace is, in contrast with all this, rightly described by the word "reconciliation"—reconciliation of men first with God and thereafter and by consequence with one another. For the fruit of the Spirit is love, joy, peace; and the transition to this from our world of enmity, misery and strife can only be by reconciliation.

The divisions and hostilities among men are the consequence of their pride and selfishness and are God's judgment upon these; for those consequences which follow from our actions or characters by the operation of God's laws are His judgments upon us. That divine judgment aims at warning us from our selfish ways; but it is never purposeless. It is the prerogative of God to bring good out of evil; and while in the conditions of this life, the only life we know, the opposites are necessary to each other and good is known chiefly in its opposition to evil, it is also true that the evil itself when overcome and merged in the good which conquers it is seen in retrospect as a contributory factor in the production of a greater good than would have come into being without it. The world whose history has as its focus the Cross and Resurrection of Jesus Christ would be a poorer, not a richer world, if the powers of evil had not led Christ to the Cross.

God can so conquer evil as to make it an instrument in the fulfilment of His purpose.

So it can be with the divisions of mankind. They spring, so far as they are real divisions, from the pride which is mingled with the varied talents and aptitudes of men, or with the enjoyment of the products of those aptitudes or talents. Thus in the old legend

Lamech has two wives, Adah and Zillah, names which probably mean *Light* and *Shadow,* and from them are born Jabal, the father of all who dwell in tents; Jubal, the father of such as handle harp and pipe; and Tubal-cain, the wielder or forger of all instruments of copper and iron. And these three, the father of the Pastoral Life, the Maker of Music and the Forger of Weapons, have a sister Na'amah, *gracious* or *beautiful,* whom later legend calls the mother of singing.

Now, how does the Song of Lamech greet all this progress of equipment and adorning of human life? With an outburst of praise to God the giver? With some apostrophe to man's power and skill? With thankful notes for the peace of the pastoral life defended by weapons from its foes? With none of these; but with a savage exultation in the fresh power of vengeance which all the novel instruments have placed in their inventors' hands.

> "Then said Lamech to his wives Adah and Zillah,
> Hearken to my voice,
> Give ear to my saying:
> I have slain a man for the hurt done me
> And a young man for the wound of me.
> If seven times Cain be avenged
> Lamech shall be seventy times seven."

How weird is this: how terrible! The first results of civilisation are to equip hatred and render revenge more deadly. And all the more weird is the little fragment, that out of those far-off days it seems to mock us with some grotesque reflection of our own time. Civilisation finding its apotheosis in enormous armaments; wealth and prosperity leading people to an arrogant clamour for war.

The little fragment is still more weirdly apposite to-day than when George Adam Smith wrote that comment upon it which I have just read, now forty-two years ago.

And, in the rivalry and the enmities, the varieties among men have blossomed into the rich endowment of the civilisation we have inherited. War itself, the most diabolical expression of the divisions among men, gives rise to feats of courage and endurance which become an inspiration not only to the nation from which each hero came, but to all mankind. God does not desert the world which He created. He is always at work within it, bringing judgment upon all the deeds of man, but with and through that judgment, blessing.

So the nations have developed through their differences from one another, and even through their conflicts, a wealth of inheritance for the civilised world which certainly has come to us through those channels and perhaps could not have been so richly developed otherwise. But the great need of our time is to find the power which shall gather all this diversity into a harmony where every distinct element has its place yet the whole is a unity, and rivalry never becomes conflict.

"We do hear them speak in our tongues the wonderful works of God." That was the Pentecostal experience. It was under the impulse of the Holy Spirit that the Apostles spoke, and the theme of their utterance was the works of God. Only so can the curse of Babel be reversed. Man must abandon his proud self-sufficiency and seek the guidance of the Spirit of God; and the theme which alone can bring all into harmony is, not their own achievements, their own cultures, their own traditions, but the wonderful works of God.

It was on such an errand of reconciliation that the Church was sent forth on its age-long pilgrimage. During its history we can see the working of its power to draw men into unity, then new outbreaks of divisiveness leading on the one hand to strife and on the other to still richer variety of human experience, and then once more the influence of the Church in unification. Wherever Christian people are with one accord in one place they can so speak of the wonderful works of God that all men of all traditions hear and understand.

It can be so to-day. It is so already to an extent that amazes those who know the facts. The actual fellowship of Christians of various ecclesiastical traditions and of almost all nations, including those at war with one another, is the supreme spiritual fact of our epoch. Chinese and Japanese; American, British and German; so far as we acknowledge the Lordship of Jesus Christ and turn our thoughts to the wonderful works wrought by God in Him, we find ourselves united at a level of experience deeper than the estrangements even of this war. Here is the greatest hope for the future. We shall need political contrivances, and Christians should to the utmost extent exercise their minds on the problems involved so that Christian influence may tell in the fashioning of the outward structure of international life when the war is over. But that structure can in any case be no more than machinery. The vital matter is the spirit which will both keep the machine at work and will also direct it to the accomplishment of certain ends and the repudiation of others.

Here the responsibility of the Christian fellowship is very great. We are the trustees of the great secret; we are called to be witnesses to those truths which are the well-spring of reconciling and unifying power. It is not in ourselves nor in our several ecclesiastical traditions that we find this power; it is in the wonderful works of God. Our address to the nations as members of the Church of Christ planted within them and among them must always be, "We preach not ourselves, but Christ Jesus as Lord and ourselves as your servants for Jesus' sake. . . . God was in Christ reconciling the world unto Himself. . . . We are ambassadors therefore on behalf of Christ, as though God were intreating by us; we beseech you on behalf of Christ, be ye reconciled to God." Only as we come to Him shall we draw near in heart to one another; only as together we seek pardon at the foot of the Cross shall we become channels of His renewing and re-creative power.

The wonderful works of God which we proclaim are supremely His redemptive acts in Jesus Christ Our Lord; to proclaim those acts is to fulfil the ministry of reconciliation committed to us. But it must be done with faith, that is with the confident expectation, born of real trust in God, that those who are reconciled to God will find themselves thereby reconciled to one another. And this means mutual forgiveness. In that savage song of Lamech which we recalled a few moments ago there were words that evoked an echo from a time far in the future when Lamech spoke: "if Cain be avenged seven times, Lamech shall be seventy times seven". Seven times! Seventy times seven! "How oft shall my brother sin against me and I forgive him?"

We do our duty as we see it, and this may involve the infliction upon our fellow men of very fearful suffering; and we brace ourselves to bear such suffering if duty calls us to endure it. Only so in the state of things which has arisen can a hideous evil be driven from the seat of power which it has usurped and the world be set free to follow again the way of fellowship. And if it is our duty to fight, it is certainly our duty to fight effectively. But we must guard our souls from the temptation which this inevitably brings. Our word of reconciliation is a word of mutual forgiveness unto seventy times seven.

Here, then, we are assembled with one accord in one place; may the Spirit of the Living and Loving God come mightily upon us that we may proclaim His wonderful works to all nations so that they shall hear and heed.

Let us then stand together and join in the Affirmation of our Unity in Christ.

XXV

Endurance and Dedication

BROADCAST ON FRIDAY, SEPTEMBER 3RD, 1943

He that endureth to the end, the same shall be saved.
St. Mark xiii. 13

YES, but to the end of what? We know that in this war there may be very much to endure. Our thankfulness for the brighter news, the nearer hope of victory and peace, must not blind us to the greatness of the task still to be accomplished before the evil powers which have taken possession of Germany and Japan are beaten and crushed. We all know that. The end, in the sense of the end of the war, is not yet, and there may be much to endure before we reach it. And we are all determined to endure till then.

But because the news is brighter, and victory and peace are nearer, I want to ask you to look beyond the war and think what is needed if the fruit of victory is to be gathered. We have all heard it said that last time we won the war and lost the peace; and even though we cannot simply endorse that description of what happened, we know what it means and we know that the aftermath of the earlier war was full of disappointment. It was partly due to lack of preparation; to make a good settlement after the upheaval of war needs as much preparation as war itself. The Government has taken steps. At least it can be said that the chief elements in the problem, international and domestic, have been surveyed, and in various reports the material is available for the formation of a public opinion and the outline of a comprehensive policy. But the cause of disappointment last time was not only or chiefly political; and if we are to hope for better things this time, it must not be through trust in improved political devices. In what spirit are we hoping for peace? Shall we enter on it ready to endure to the end, or shall we look forward only to rest, relaxation and enjoyment of a life as like as possible to what we knew before the war without its insecurity? Our preparation for peace must be spiritual as well as political if we are this time to win the peace; and the spiritual preparation is vastly the more important of the two, though both are necessary, because if the right spirit is lacking no political contrivances can save us from renewed disaster; and if the spirit is right it will devise the right machinery.

The spirit that we shall need, then as now, is the spirit of dedication. Of course we may rightly look forward to some measure of rest from the labour and strain which must not be relaxed till victory is won. But the establishment of peace will not be the inauguration of a period of ease and plenty. Boundless wealth has been destroyed in the war; there will be shortage of food, of the means of raising food and of many materials of industry. We shall need in a very special degree both hard work to replenish the world's exhausted stores, and unselfishness in the distribution and use of them, if the peace is to be true peace. This means a great need still for discipline, corporate discipline and self-discipline. By sacrifice and endurance we hope to win the war. Let us recognise, and root in our minds the conviction, that only by continued endurance and sacrifice can we win the peace.

The war has taught us many lessons. One of these has been the truth that we and all men are members one of another.

There is for all the world one weal and one woe. Peace and war alike are one and indivisible. No nation in the modern world can have assured prosperity unless all nations prosper. Once and for all we must set ourselves to abandon the selfish aim of a prosperity won against impoverished rivals. We must learn to believe in an altogether new way in the family of mankind.

One way of describing what this war is all about is to say that the Germans and Japanese believe in unity imposed by master races on subject races. We fight to prevent that. But when we have prevented that, the chief part of our task remains to be accomplished—the use of our power to establish, not our own supremacy, but true fellowship for all, with freedom for the backward races to advance, and for all to develop their own manner of life according to the various gifts which God has given them.

For the victorious nations will have great power; and if they use it selfishly no political devices can prevent the generation of forces ready to explode in yet another war. If we want peace on any other than the German model, it must rest on freedom and justice, and so much curtailment of our exercise of freedom as justice to all may at any time require.

Now it is easy enough to say all this, and to assent to it when others say it. But it is going to happen only if each of us in all his dealings is dedicated to the task. In our family life, needing in so many cases to be built up again after the scattering of its members by the claims of war, in our action as Trade Unionists or as Directors of Companies, in our influence as citizens upon the policy of the State at home and abroad, we shall need the spirit of dedication to be supreme, not the spirit of self-seeking. It has often been noticed how even men who are very unselfish in personal affairs become utterly selfish when they act as a group—as Directors of a Company or as Trade Unionists, for instance. Half our troubles come from this. Yet when all is said, the chief way for each of us to bring about a better world is the simple one of living a better life—more honest, more pure, more self-controlled, more generous.

Where are we to find the power for this re-direction of our energies? For we now see that the end unto which we must endure is for each of us the end of life and for all of us beyond the end of each one's life; it is the end of all things, the consummation of history in the fulfilment of the purpose of God. We need, then, a dedication without limit in either time or space. It will fail, and consequently we shall fail, if it is anything other or less than dedication to God.

We human beings are selfish folk; and when we are tired we tend to be more selfish than ever. We shall not find strength in ourselves to dedicate our lives with the completeness which is demanded; we must seek it in our prayers. This is a day of prayer and dedication; and our very prayer must be for the power to dedicate ourselves. We make it in the name of Him whose dedication was complete, "Who for the joy that was set before Him"—the joy of a world by Him redeemed from the misery of selfishness into the blessedness of love—"endured the Cross".

The throne of the united world is not a Chair of State; its emblems are not sceptre, orb and sword; it is a Cross and the Crown is made of thorns. It is as worshippers at the Cross of Christ that we set ourselves to win for the world true peace.